BEST PILLSBURY RECIPES

WILEY

John Wiley & Sons, Inc.

Library of Congress Cataloging-in-Publication Data is available upon request.

ISBN: 978-1-435-13969-5 (pbk)

Manufactured in China

10 9 8 7 6 5 4 3 2 1

GENERAL MILLS

Editorial Director: *Jeff Nowak*

Manager and Editor, Cookbooks: *Lois Tlusty*

Recipe Development and Testing: *Pillsbury Kitchens*

Photography: *General Mills Photography Studios and Image Library*

JOHN WILEY & SONS, INC.

Publisher: *Natalie Chapman*

Executive Editor: *Anne Ficklen*

Production Editor: *Abby Saul*

Cover Design: *Suzanne Sunwoo*

Art Director: *Tai Blanche*

Interior Design and Layout: *Indianapolis Composition Services*

Manufacturing Manager: *Tom Hyland*

For more great recipes visit **pillsbury.com**

Dear Friends,

Come and enjoy our best recipes—you are going to love them. Why are they our best? Well, they are easy to make, fun to eat and make putting meals on the table a snap. What's not to like?

We have you covered from breakfast through dinner, plus we included great recipes for entertaining, holidays and just-for-fun time, like Rocky Road S'more Bars for a TGIF treat or French Toast Strata for a lazy Sunday morning. We know you love great food, and we have all the best recipes for you right here.

Who couldn't use some more dinner ideas? Try Classic Chicken Pot Pie, Basil-Pork and Asian Noodles, Sloppy Joe Confetti Tacos or Foot-Long Pizza—all give you dinner in just one dish. It doesn't get easier—or tastier than that.

Want dinner fast? Speed ahead with Orange Chicken Stir-fry, Grilled Marinated Shrimp or Turkey Meat Loaves. And don't forget dessert! You'll love Dixie Spice Cake with Caramel Frosting, Apple Pie Foldovers, Individual Mixed-Berry Pies, Soft-and-Chewy Chocolate Chip Cookies and Frosted Irish Cream Brownies.

Dig in—you'll love the recipes here!

Sincerely,
The Pillsbury Editors

Contents

Cheesy Potato and Sausage Frittata 8 • Apple–Canadian Bacon Omelet 10 • Home-Style Sausage and Potato Skillet 12 • Scrambled Egg and Veggie Pockets 14 • Cheddar-Chive Drop Biscuits 16 • French Toast with Raspberry-Cranberry Syrup 18 • Cinnamon-Oat Scones 20 • Chocolate-Hazelnut Breakfast Ring 22 • Crunchy Trail Mix Bars 24 • Banana Bread 26 • Whole Wheat Bread 28

CHAPTER 1

Breakfasts
and Breads

Cheesy Potato and Sausage Frittata

START TO FINISH 35 MINUTES
4 SERVINGS

6 oz. bulk light turkey and pork sausage

4 cups frozen potatoes O'Brien with onions and peppers (from 28-oz. bag)

1 cup fat-free cholesterol-free egg product (from 8-oz. carton) or 4 eggs, lightly beaten

¼ cup fat-free (skim) milk

⅛ teaspoon ground red pepper (cayenne)

⅛ teaspoon pepper

⅛ teaspoon fennel seed, crushed, if desired

½ cup finely shredded reduced-fat Cheddar cheese (2 oz.)

1 Heat 12-inch nonstick skillet over high heat. Add sausage; cook 4 to 5 minutes, stirring frequently, until no longer pink. Remove sausage from skillet; drain on paper towels. Return sausage to skillet. Gently stir in potatoes.

2 In small bowl, mix egg product and remaining ingredients except cheese until well blended. Pour egg mixture evenly over potato mixture; cover and cook over medium-low heat 10 minutes.

3 Uncover; cook 5 to 8 minutes longer or until egg product mixture is set but still moist on top. Remove from heat. Sprinkle cheese over top. Let stand until cheese is melted, 3 to 5 minutes. Cut into wedges to serve.

1 SERVING: Calories 300; Total Fat 9g (Saturated Fat 3.5g; Trans Fat 0g); Cholesterol 35mg; Sodium 710mg; Total Carbohydrate 36g (Dietary Fiber 4g; Sugars 3g)

EXCHANGES: 2½ Starch, 2 Lean Meat

CARBOHYDRATE CHOICES: 2½

Apple–Canadian Bacon Omelet

START TO FINISH 20 MINUTES
4 SERVINGS

4 teaspoons butter or margarine

2 medium Golden Delicious apples, peeled, cut into thin wedges (about 2 cups)

4 oz. Canadian bacon (about 6 slices), cut into thin strips

2 tablespoons real maple syrup

1½ cups fat-free cholesterol-free egg product (from two 8-oz. cartons) or 4 whole eggs plus 4 egg whites, lightly beaten

⅛ teaspoon pepper

1 In 8-inch nonstick skillet or 2-quart saucepan, melt 1 teaspoon of the butter over medium heat. Add apple; cook about 5 minutes, stirring occasionally, until crisp-tender. Stir in Canadian bacon. Reduce heat to medium-low; cook and stir about 2 minutes. Remove from heat. Stir in syrup.

2 Meanwhile, in medium bowl, mix egg product or beaten eggs and egg whites and the pepper until well blended.

3 In 10-inch nonstick skillet with flared sides (omelet pan), melt remaining 3 teaspoons butter over medium heat. Pour egg mixture into skillet. Cook about 1 minute, lifting edges occasionally to allow uncooked egg mixture to flow to bottom of skillet, until mixture begins to cook around edges. Reduce heat to medium-low; cover and cook 3 to 6 minutes or until set.

4 Spoon half of filling over half of omelet; quickly fold other half of omelet over filling. Cut omelet in half; slide each half onto serving plate. Spoon remaining filling over each serving.

1 SERVING: Calories 210; Total Fat 6g (Saturated Fat 3g; Trans Fat 0g); Cholesterol 25mg; Sodium 680mg; Total Carbohydrate 19g (Dietary Fiber 2g; Sugars 15g)

EXCHANGES: ½ Fruit, ½ Other Carbohydrate, 2½ Very Lean Meat, 1 Fat

CARBOHYDRATE CHOICES: 1

Home-Style Sausage and Potato Skillet

START TO FINISH 30 MINUTES
4 SERVINGS (1¼ CUPS EACH)

¾ lb bulk light turkey and pork sausage

1 large or 2 medium onions, chopped (1 cup)

2 lb red potatoes (about 12 medium), unpeeled, very thinly sliced

1 cup water

½ teaspoon salt

½ teaspoon paprika

¼ teaspoon dried thyme leaves

⅛ teaspoon pepper

1 Heat nonstick skillet over medium-high heat. Add sausage; cook 4 to 5 minutes, stirring frequently, until no longer pink. Remove sausage from Dutch oven; drain on paper towels. Set aside.

2 Wipe Dutch oven clean with paper towels. Add onions; cook over medium heat about 5 minutes, stirring occasionally.

3 Gently stir in cooked sausage and remaining ingredients. Heat to boiling. Reduce heat to medium-low; cover tightly and cook 8 to 10 minutes, stirring occasionally, just until potatoes are tender.

4 Remove from heat; gently stir mixture. Let stand covered 10 minutes to allow flavors to blend and light sauce to form.

1 SERVING: Calories 360; Total Fat 9g (Saturated Fat 2g; Trans Fat 0g); Cholesterol 80mg; Sodium 880mg; Total Carbohydrate 44g (Dietary Fiber 6g)

EXCHANGES: 3 Starch, 2 Lean Meat

CARBOHYDRATE CHOICES: 3

Scrambled Egg and Veggie Pockets

START TO FINISH 20 MINUTES
4 SANDWICHES

1 carton (8 oz) fat-free egg product (1 cup) or 4 eggs, lightly beaten

½ cup shredded American cheese (2 oz)

½ teaspoon onion powder

1 tablespoon butter or margarine

1 cup chopped broccoli

½ cup shredded carrot

¼ cup chopped red or green bell pepper

2 tablespoons sliced ripe olives

2 pita (pocket) breads (6 inch), cut in half to form pockets

1 In medium bowl, mix egg product, cheese and onion powder; set aside.

2 In 10-inch skillet, melt butter over medium heat. Add broccoli, carrot, bell pepper and olives; cook 3 to 5 minutes, stirring frequently, until vegetables are crisp-tender.

3 Pour egg mixture over vegetables; reduce heat to low. Cook, stirring occasionally from outside edge to center, allowing uncooked egg mixture to flow to bottom of skillet, until center is set but still moist.

4 Spoon egg mixture evenly into pita bread halves.

1 SANDWICH: Calories 200; Total Fat 8g (Saturated Fat 4.5g; Trans Fat 0g); Cholesterol 20mg; Sodium 530mg; Total Carbohydrate 19g (Dietary Fiber 2g)

EXCHANGES: 1 Starch, 1 Vegetable, 1 Lean Meat, 1 Fat

CARBOHYDRATE CHOICES: 1

The veggies add lots of crunch and lots of vitamins and minerals to this easy, colorful dinner. Use your family's favorites or any veggies on hand.

Cheddar-Chive Drop Biscuits

START TO FINISH 30 MINUTES
18 BISCUITS

2 cups all-purpose flour

3 teaspoons baking powder

1 teaspoon salt

½ cup shortening

1¼ cups plain yogurt

1 cup shredded Cheddar
    cheese (4 oz.)

¼ cup chopped fresh chives

1 Heat oven to 450°F. Grease large cookie sheet with shortening or cooking spray. In large bowl, mix flour, baking powder and salt. With pastry blender or fork, cut in shortening until mixture resembles coarse crumbs. Stir in yogurt, cheese and chives just until moistened.

2 Drop dough by generous tablespoonfuls onto cookie sheet.

3 Bake 9 to 12 minutes or until light golden brown. Serve warm.

1 BISCUIT: Calories 140; Total Fat 8g (Saturated Fat 3g; Trans Fat 1g); Cholesterol 10mg; Sodium 260mg; Total Carbohydrate 12g (Dietary Fiber 0g; Sugars 1g)

EXCHANGES: 1 Starch, 1½ Fat

CARBOHYDRATE CHOICES: 1

Stir gently and work quickly to get the most tender biscuits. Stirring just until all the dry ingredients are moistened keeps the biscuits from becoming tough.

French Toast with Raspberry-Cranberry Syrup

START TO FINISH 40 MINUTES
4 SERVINGS

FRENCH TOAST

2 whole eggs plus 1 egg white, lightly beaten, or ½ cup fat-free cholesterol-free egg product (from 8-oz. carton)

1 cup fat-free (skim) milk

2 teaspoons rum extract

¼ teaspoon ground nutmeg

8 slices (1 inch thick) French bread

SYRUP

½ cup frozen (thawed) raspberry blend juice concentrate

½ cup jellied cranberry sauce

1 tablespoon powdered sugar

1 Heat oven to 425°F. In medium bowl, mix beaten eggs and egg white, the milk, rum extract and nutmeg until well blended.

2 Dip bread slices into egg mixture, coating both sides well. Place in ungreased 11×7-inch (2-quart) glass baking dish. Pour remaining eggnog mixture over bread slices. Let stand at room temperature 15 minutes.

3 Spray cookie sheet with cooking spray. Remove bread slices from dish; place on cookie sheet. Bake 12 to 15 minutes or until golden brown, turning slices once halfway through baking.

4 In 1-quart saucepan, mix syrup ingredients; cook over medium-low heat, stirring occasionally, until cranberry sauce and sugar have melted. Serve French toast with syrup.

1 SERVING: Calories 300; Total Fat 4.5g (Saturated Fat 1.5g; Trans Fat 0g); Cholesterol 105mg; Sodium 340mg; Total Carbohydrate 55g (Dietary Fiber 2g; Sugars 32g)

EXCHANGES: 1½ Starch, 2 Other Carbohydrate, 1 Medium-Fat Meat

CARBOHYDRATE CHOICES: 3½

Cinnamon-Oat Scones

START TO FINISH: 1 HOUR
8 SCONES

SCONES

1½ cups all-purpose flour

¾ cup oats

¼ cup packed brown sugar

2 teaspoons baking powder

½ teaspoon salt

½ teaspoon ground cinnamon

½ cup butter or margarine

½ cup milk

TOPPING

1 tablespoon butter or
  margarine, melted

1 tablespoon granulated
  sugar

¼ teaspoon ground cinnamon

1 Heat oven to 375°F. Lightly grease cookie sheet with shortening or cooking spray. In medium bowl, mix flour, oats, brown sugar, baking powder, salt and ½ teaspoon cinnamon. With pastry blender or fork, cut in ½ cup butter until mixture is crumbly. Add milk all at once; stir just until dry ingredients are moistened.

2 On floured work surface, gently knead dough 5 or 6 times. Place on cookie sheet; press into 6-inch round, about 1 inch thick. Brush top with melted butter.

3 In small bowl, mix granulated sugar and ¼ teaspoon cinnamon. Sprinkle over top. Cut into 8 wedges; separate slightly.

4 Bake 20 to 30 minutes or until golden brown. Serve warm.

1 SCONE: Calories 270; Total Fat 14g (Saturated Fat 7g; Trans Fat 1g); Cholesterol 35mg; Sodium 370mg; Total Carbohydrate 32g (Dietary Fiber 2g; Sugars 9g)

EXCHANGES: 1½ Starch, ½ Other Carbohydrate, 2½ Fat

CARBOHYDRATE CHOICES: 2

Chocolate-Hazelnut Breakfast Ring

START TO FINISH 40 MINUTES
8 SERVINGS

1 can (13.8 oz.) refrigerated pizza crust

⅔ cup hazelnut spread with cocoa (from 13-oz. jar), stirred to soften

½ cup whole hazelnuts (filberts), toasted, finely chopped

1 egg, beaten

½ teaspoon granulated sugar

1 teaspoon powdered sugar

1 Heat oven to 350°F. Line cookie sheet with cooking parchment paper. On lightly floured work surface, unroll dough; press into 13×10-inch rectangle. Gently spread hazelnut spread to within ½ inch of edges. Sprinkle with toasted hazelnuts.

2 Fold long sides of dough over filling to meet in center. Starting with 1 long side, loosely roll up dough. Shape dough roll into ring on cookie sheet; pinch ends together to seal. Cut 5 (1-inch-deep) slits in top of dough. Brush with beaten egg; sprinkle with granulated sugar.

3 Bake 20 to 25 minutes or until golden brown. Remove from cookie sheet; place on serving platter. Cool 10 minutes before serving. Sprinkle with powdered sugar; serve warm.

1 SERVING: Calories 320; Total Fat 14g (Saturated Fat 1.5g; Trans Fat 0g); Cholesterol 25mg; Sodium 370mg; Total Carbohydrate 41g (Dietary Fiber 2g; Sugars 18g)

EXCHANGES: 2 Starch, ½ Other Carbohydrate, 2½ Fat

CARBOHYDRATE CHOICES: 3

To toast whole hazelnuts, spread them on a cookie sheet and bake at 375°F for 5 to 8 minutes or until golden brown.

Crunchy Trail Mix Bars

START TO FINISH 30 MINUTES
36 BARS

4 cups Cheerios® cereal

3 cups trail mix (seeds, nuts and dried fruits)

¼ cup butter or margarine

1 cup packed brown sugar

2 tablespoons all-purpose flour

½ cup light corn syrup

1 Grease 13×9-inch pan with shortening, or spray with cooking spray. In large bowl, mix cereal and trail mix; set aside.

2 In 2-quart saucepan, melt butter over medium heat. Stir in brown sugar, flour and corn syrup. Cook, stirring occasionally, until mixture comes to a full boil. Boil 1 minute, stirring constantly.

3 Pour mixture evenly over cereal mixture; toss to coat. Press mixture in pan. Cool 10 minutes. For bars, cut into 6 rows by 6 rows.

1 BAR: Calories 130; Total Fat 5g (Saturated Fat 1.5g; Trans Fat 0g); Cholesterol 0mg; Sodium 65mg; Total Carbohydrate 18g (Dietary Fiber 1g)

EXCHANGES: ½ Starch, ½ Other Carbohydrate, 1 Fat

CARBOHYDRATE CHOICES: 1

If you plan to bring these to a gathering, cut them into bars and place on a large plastic or paper plate, then cover with plastic wrap or foil for toting. You won't need to carry the pan home!

Banana Bread

START TO FINISH 2 HOURS 20 MINUTES
1 LOAF; 16 SLICES

¾ cup sugar

½ cup butter or margarine, softened

2 eggs

1 cup mashed ripe bananas (2 medium)

⅓ cup milk

1 teaspoon vanilla

2 cups all-purpose flour

½ cup chopped nuts, if desired

1 teaspoon baking soda

½ teaspoon salt

1 Heat oven to 350°F. Grease bottom only of 9×5- or 8×4-inch loaf pan with shortening or cooking spray. In large bowl, beat sugar and butter with spoon until light and fluffy. Beat in eggs. Stir in bananas, milk and vanilla until well blended.

2 In small bowl, mix flour, nuts, baking soda and salt. Add to banana mixture all at once; stir just until dry ingredients are moistened. Pour into pan.

3 Bake 50 to 60 minutes or until toothpick inserted in center comes out clean. Cool 5 minutes; remove from pan. Cool completely, about 1 hour. Wrap tightly and store in refrigerator.

1 SLICE: Calories 170; Total Fat 7g (Saturated Fat 3g; Trans Fat 0g); Cholesterol 40mg; Sodium 200mg; Total Carbohydrate 25g (Dietary Fiber 0g; Sugars 11g)

EXCHANGES: 1 Starch, ½ Other Carbohydrate, 1½ Fat

CARBOHYDRATE CHOICES: 1½

VARIATIONS:

Applesauce Bread: Substitute 1 cup applesauce for mashed bananas; stir ¾ teaspoon ground cinnamon into flour mixture.

Berry-Banana Bread: Stir ½ cup sweetened dried cranberries into flour mixture.

Currant-Banana Bread: Stir ½ cup dried currants into flour mixture.

Whole Wheat Bread

START TO FINISH 3 HOURS 50 MINUTES
2 LOAVES; 16 SLICES EACH

2 packages regular active
 dry yeast

¼ cup warm water
 (105°F to 115°F)

½ cup packed brown sugar
 or honey

¼ cup butter or margarine

3 teaspoons salt

2½ cups hot water

4½ cups whole wheat flour

2¾ to 3¾ cups all-purpose
 flour

1 In small bowl, dissolve yeast in warm water. In large bowl, mix brown sugar, butter, salt and hot water; cool 5 minutes.

2 To cooled brown sugar mixture, beat in 3 cups of the whole wheat flour with electric mixer on low speed until moistened, scraping bowl frequently. Beat on medium speed 3 minutes, scraping bowl frequently. Beat in remaining 1½ cups whole wheat flour and the dissolved yeast. With spoon, stir in 2¼ to 2¾ cups of the all-purpose flour until dough pulls cleanly away from side of bowl.

3 On floured work surface, knead in remaining ½ to 1 cup all-purpose flour until dough is smooth and elastic, 10 to 15 minutes. Grease large bowl with shortening or cooking spray. Place dough in bowl; cover loosely with plastic wrap and cloth towel. Let rise in warm place (80°F to 85°F) 30 to 45 minutes or until light and doubled in size.

4 Generously grease 2 (8×4- or 9×5-inch) loaf pans with shortening or cooking spray. Gently push fist into dough to deflate; divide in half. On lightly floured work surface, roll out each half of dough with rolling pin into 18×8-inch rectangle. Starting with one 8-inch side, roll up dough tightly, pressing with thumbs to seal after each turn. Pinch edge of dough into roll to seal; press each end with side of hand to seal. Fold ends under loaf; place seam side down in pan. Cover; let rise in warm place 30 to 45 minutes or until light and doubled in size.

5 Heat oven to 375°F. Uncover dough; bake 30 minutes. Reduce oven temperature to 350°F; bake 10 to 15 minutes longer or until loaves sound hollow when lightly tapped. Immediately remove from pans; place on wire racks. Cool completely, about 1 hour.

1 SLICE: Calories 130; Total Fat 2g (Saturated Fat 1g; Trans Fat 0g); Cholesterol 0mg; Sodium 230mg; Total Carbohydrate 24g (Dietary Fiber 2g; Sugars 3g)

EXCHANGES: 1½ Starch

CARBOHYDRATE CHOICES: 1½

Chipotle Pico de Gallo 32 • Garlic Cream and Tomato
Crostini 34 • Crispy Shrimp Tarts 36 • Caprese Salad Kabobs 38 •
Margarita Shot-Glass Shrimp 40 • Jerk Chicken Wings
with Creamy Dipping Sauce 42 • Meatballs with Fire-Roasted
Tomato Sauce 44 • Cheeseburger Bites 46 •
Almond-Parmesan Asparagus 48 • Orange-Glazed Carrots
and Sugar Snap Peas 50 • Creamy Marinated Potato Salad 52 •
Orzo-Barley Pilaf 54

CHAPTER 2

Appetizers

and Sides

Chipotle Pico de Gallo

START TO FINISH: 40 MINUTES
12 SERVINGS (3 CUPS)

1 cup coarsely chopped
  unpeeled seedless
  cucumber

½ cup chopped peeled jicama

½ cup chopped red bell
  pepper

1 tablespoon lime juice

1 tablespoon honey

¼ teaspoon salt

2 seedless oranges, peeled,
  coarsely chopped

2 chipotle chiles in adobo
  sauce (from a can),
  chopped

12 oz whole-grain tortilla
  chips

1 In medium bowl, mix all ingredients except chips.

2 Serve immediately with chips, or cover and refrigerate until serving time.

1 SERVING (¼ CUP): Calories 160; Total Fat 6g (Saturated Fat 0.5g; Trans Fat 0g); Cholesterol 0mg; Sodium 180mg; Total Carbohydrate 25g (Dietary Fiber 3g)

EXCHANGES: 1 Starch, ½ Other Carbohydrate, 1 Fat

CARBOHYDRATE CHOICES: 1½

This smoky pico de gallo is excellent with grilled chicken, fish or pork. To turn up the heat, add more adobo. To make this relish less spicy, use just one chipotle chile.

Garlic Cream and Tomato Crostini

START TO FINISH 15 MINUTES
20 CROSTINI

20 slices French bread
  (½ inch)

1 tablespoon olive or
  vegetable oil

½ cup garlic-and-herb cream
  cheese spread (from 8-oz
  container)

4 medium green onions,
  chopped (¼ cup)

1 tablespoon chopped fresh
  thyme leaves

2 medium fresh plum (Roma)
  tomatoes, chopped

1 Set oven control to broil. On ungreased cookie sheet, place bread slices. Lightly brush each with oil. Broil with tops 4 to 6 inches from heat about 1 minute or until light golden brown.

2 In small bowl, mix cream cheese and green onions. Spread mixture on toasted bread slices. Broil about 1 minute longer or until cream cheese bubbles. Sprinkle thyme leaves and tomatoes over top.

1 CROSTINI: Calories 50; Total Fat 3g (Saturated Fat 1.5g; Trans Fat 0g); Cholesterol 5mg; Sodium 70mg; Total Carbohydrate 5g (Dietary Fiber 0g)

EXCHANGES: ½ Starch, ½ Fat

CARBOHYDRATE CHOICES: ½

Garlic-and-herb cream cheese spread is soft cream cheese found near the regular cream cheese in the grocery store.

To make ahead, toast bread, and cool completely before storing in an airtight food-storage plastic bag. Just before serving, spread crostini with cream cheese mixture, and broil.

Crispy Shrimp Tarts

START TO FINISH: 55 MINUTES
24 APPETIZERS

24 frozen mini fillo shells
(from two 2.1-oz packages)

½ cup cream cheese spread
(from 8-oz container)

24 frozen cooked deveined
peeled medium shrimp

¼ cup Chinese plum sauce

Grated lime peel, if desired

1 Heat oven to 350°F. Place fillo shells on ungreased large cookie sheet.

2 Stir cream cheese to soften. Spoon 1 teaspoon cream cheese into each shell. Top each with 1 shrimp.

3 Bake about 2 minutes or until cream cheese is soft. Remove from cookie sheet; place on serving platter. Top each with ½ teaspoon plum sauce and lime peel.

1 APPETIZER: Calories 40; Total Fat 2.5g (Saturated Fat 1g; Trans Fat 0g); Cholesterol 15mg; Sodium 60mg; Total Carbohydrate 3g (Dietary Fiber 0g)

EXCHANGES: 1/2 Medium-Fat Meat

CARBOHYDRATE CHOICES: 0

Cooked crabmeat can be used in place of the shrimp.

Caprese Salad Kabobs

START TO FINISH 30 MINUTES
34 KABOBS

¼ cup extra-virgin olive oil

2 tablespoons lemon juice

⅔ cup coarsely chopped fresh basil leaves or lemon basil leaves

¼ teaspoon salt

¼ teaspoon freshly ground black pepper

1 pint (2 cups) red cherry tomatoes

1 pint (2 cups) yellow cherry tomatoes

2 medium zucchini or yellow summer squash, cubed

1 lb fresh mozzarella cheese, cubed

34 (6-inch) bamboo skewers

Fresh basil leaves, if desired

1 In large bowl, mix oil, lemon juice, basil, salt and pepper, using wire whisk. Add tomatoes, zucchini and cheese. Cover and refrigerate 10 minutes.

2 Drain vegetables, reserving olive oil mixture. Thread skewers alternately with tomatoes, zucchini and cheese; top with basil leaf. Serve kabobs with reserved olive oil mixture.

1 KABOB: Calories 60; Total Fat 4.5g (Saturated Fat 2g; Trans Fat 0g); Cholesterol 5mg; Sodium 90mg; Total Carbohydrate 2g (Dietary Fiber 0g)

EXCHANGES: ½ Vegetable, 1 Fat

CARBOHYDRATE CHOICES: 0

Virtually any skewer-able vegetable will work in this recipe. Try red, green or yellow bell pepper pieces or fresh pea pods.

Make ahead for even more flavor.

Margarita Shot-Glass Shrimp

START TO FINISH 30 MINUTES
24 APPETIZERS

Lime wedges, if desired

Coarse salt, if desired

Coarse ground black pepper, if desired

1 cup zesty cocktail sauce

½ cup finely chopped red or yellow bell pepper

1 tablespoon lime juice

2 cans (8 oz each) crushed pineapple in juice, drained

24 cooked deveined peeled large shrimp (about 2 lb)

Cilantro sprigs, if desired

1 Rub rims of 24 (2-oz) cordial glasses (shot glasses) with lime wedges; dip rims in coarse salt and pepper.

2 In medium bowl, mix cocktail sauce, bell pepper, lime juice and pineapple. Place about 1 tablespoon sauce mixture in bottom of each glass. Place 1 shrimp in each glass; top each with lime wedge and cilantro sprig. Serve immediately, or cover and refrigerate until serving time.

Alternative Method: In medium bowl, mix cocktail sauce, bell pepper, lime juice and pineapple. Serve immediately, or cover and refrigerate until serving time. To serve, spoon cocktail sauce mixture into small serving bowl; place on serving tray. Arrange shrimp around bowl of sauce. Garnish with lime wedges and cilantro sprigs.

1 APPETIZER: Calories 40; Total Fat 0g (Saturated Fat 0g; Trans Fat 0g); Cholesterol 35mg; Sodium 170mg; Total Carbohydrate 5g (Dietary Fiber 0g)

EXCHANGES: ½ Other Carbohydrate, ½ Very Lean Meat

CARBOHYDRATE CHOICES: ½

Buy plastic disposable shot glasses at a party supply store if you don't have enough glass ones.

Regular seafood cocktail sauce plus ⅛ teaspoon ground red pepper (cayenne) can be used in place of the zesty cocktail sauce.

Jerk Chicken Wings with Creamy Dipping Sauce

START TO FINISH 1 HOUR 55 MINUTES
12 SERVINGS

CHICKEN WINGS

2 tablespoons dried thyme leaves

1 tablespoon packed brown sugar

1 tablespoon finely chopped garlic (3 to 4 medium cloves)

3 teaspoons ground allspice

1 teaspoon salt

2 tablespoons cider vinegar

2 tablespoons red pepper sauce

1 package (3 lb) frozen chicken wing drummettes, thawed

DIPPING SAUCE

½ cup chopped green onions (8 medium)

½ cup sour cream

½ cup mayonnaise

1 In large nonmetal bowl, mix thyme, brown sugar, garlic, allspice, salt, vinegar and pepper sauce. Add chicken wings; toss to coat evenly. Cover; refrigerate 1 hour to marinate.

2 Heat oven to 425°F. Line two 15×10×1-inch pans with foil; spray foil with cooking spray. Place chicken wings in pans; discard any remaining marinade.

3 Bake 45 minutes or until chicken is no longer pink next to bone.

4 Meanwhile, in small bowl, mix all dipping sauce ingredients.

5 Serve chicken wings with sauce.

1 SERVING: Calories 220; Total Fat 17g (Saturated Fat 4.5g; Trans Fat 0g); Cholesterol 45mg; Sodium 300mg; Total Carbohydrate 3g (Dietary Fiber 0g; Sugars 2g)

EXCHANGES: 2 Medium-Fat Meat, 1½ Fat

CARBOHYDRATE CHOICES: 0

To make ahead, bake the drummettes as directed in the recipe. Place in a covered container; refrigerate up to 24 hours. To reheat, place in a foil-lined 15×10×1-inch pan; bake at 350°F about 20 minutes or until thoroughly heated.

Meatballs with Fire-Roasted Tomato Sauce

START TO FINISH 30 MINUTES
15 SERVINGS (2 MEATBALLS EACH)

MEATBALLS

1 lb extra-lean (at least 90%) ground beef

¼ cup unseasoned dry bread crumbs

½ teaspoon garlic salt

¼ teaspoon pepper

4 medium green onions, finely chopped (¼ cup)

1 egg

SAUCE

1 jar (25.5 oz) fire-roasted tomato pasta sauce

¾ cup dried cherries, chopped

½ cup water

2 tablespoons cider vinegar or wine vinegar

Chopped fresh chives, if desired

1 Heat oven to 400°F. In large bowl, mix meatball ingredients. Shape into 30 (1-inch) meatballs. Place in ungreased 13×9-inch pan.

2 Bake uncovered about 15 minutes or until thoroughly cooked and no longer pink in center.

3 Meanwhile, in 3-quart saucepan, heat all sauce ingredients except chives to boiling, stirring occasionally; reduce heat. Stir in meatballs. Sprinkle with chives. Serve in chafing dish or slow cooker on Low heat setting.

1 SERVING: Calories 110; Total Fat 3.5g (Saturated Fat 1g; Trans Fat 0g); Cholesterol 35mg; Sodium 200mg; Total Carbohydrate 11g (Dietary Fiber 1g)

EXCHANGES: 1 Other Carbohydrate, 1 Lean Meat

CARBOHYDRATE CHOICES: 1

One can (14.5 oz) fire-roasted diced tomatoes can be used instead of the water in the sauce. Instead of toothpicks, try spearing these meatballs with pretzel sticks.

Cheeseburger Bites

START TO FINISH 3 HOURS 15 MINUTES ▪ SLOW COOKER: 3½ TO 4 QUART
24 APPETIZERS

BITES

1 lb lean (at least 80%)
   ground beef

2 tablespoons ketchup

2 teaspoons instant minced
   onion

1 teaspoon yellow mustard

8 oz American cheese loaf,
   cut into 2-inch cubes
   (2 cups)

24 miniature burger buns,
   split

TOPPINGS,
AS DESIRED

Dill pickle chips

Sliced plum (Roma) tomatoes

Shredded lettuce

Additional ketchup
   and mustard

1 In 10-inch skillet, cook beef over medium-high heat 5 to 7 minutes, stirring frequently, until thoroughly cooked; drain. Stir in 2 tablespoons ketchup, the onion and 1 teaspoon mustard.

2 Spray 3½- to 4-quart slow cooker with cooking spray. Into slow cooker, spoon beef mixture. Top with cheese.

3 Cover; cook on Low heat setting 3 to 4 hours.

4 Just before serving, stir beef mixture. Spoon 1 rounded tablespoon mixture into each bun. Serve with desired toppings.

1 APPETIZER (WITHOUT TOPPINGS): Calories 140; Total Fat 6g (Saturated Fat 3g; Trans Fat 0g); Cholesterol 20mg; Sodium 290mg; Total Carbohydrate 13g (Dietary Fiber 0g)

EXCHANGES: 1 Starch, ½ Medium-Fat Meat, ½ Fat

CARBOHYDRATE CHOICES: 1

Almond-Parmesan Asparagus

START TO FINISH 20 MINUTES
8 SERVINGS

2 tablespoons sliced almonds

2 teaspoons butter or margarine

2 teaspoons all-purpose flour

½ cup fat-free half-and-half

⅛ teaspoon salt

Dash pepper

Dash ground nutmeg, if desired

2 lb fresh asparagus spears

½ cup chopped yellow bell pepper

¼ cup shredded Parmesan cheese (1 oz)

1 In 8-inch skillet, cook almonds over medium-low heat 4 to 6 minutes, stirring frequently, until fragrant and lightly browned. Remove from skillet; set aside.

2 In same skillet, melt butter over medium-low heat. With wire whisk, stir in flour until blended. Stir in half-and-half, salt, pepper and nutmeg. Cook, stirring constantly, until mixture boils. Cook 2 to 3 minutes longer, stirring constantly, until thickened. Remove from heat; cover to keep warm.

3 Break off tough ends of asparagus spears. In 4-quart saucepan or Dutch oven, place asparagus; add ½ cup water. Heat to boiling over medium heat. Cook uncovered 3 to 5 minutes or until asparagus is crisp-tender, adding bell pepper during last minute of cooking; drain.

4 On large serving platter, arrange asparagus and bell pepper. Spoon sauce over top; sprinkle with cheese and almonds.

1 SERVING: Calories 60; Total Fat 3g (Saturated Fat 1.5g; Trans Fat 0g); Cholesterol 5mg; Sodium 125mg; Total Carbohydrate 5g (Dietary Fiber 1g)

EXCHANGES: 1 Vegetable, ½ Fat

CARBOHYDRATE CHOICES: ½

Look for fresh asparagus that is bright green with firm, unopened tips. To trim, snap off the tough ends where they break naturally. If desired, use a vegetable peeler to remove the outer layer of the spears.

Orange-Glazed Carrots and Sugar Snap Peas

START TO FINISH 15 MINUTES
6 SERVINGS (½ CUP EACH)

2 cups ready-to-eat baby-cut carrots

1 cup frozen sugar snap peas

2 tablespoons orange marmalade

¼ teaspoon salt

Dash pepper

1 In 2-quart saucepan, heat 1 cup water to boiling. Add carrots; return to boiling. Reduce heat to low; cover and simmer 8 to 10 minutes or until carrots are tender, adding sugar snap peas during last 5 minutes of cook time. Drain; return to saucepan.

2 Stir in marmalade, salt and pepper. Cook and stir over medium heat until marmalade is melted and vegetables are glazed.

1 SERVING: Calories 50; Total Fat 0g (Saturated Fat 0g; Trans Fat 0g); Cholesterol 0mg; Sodium 130mg; Total Carbohydrate 10g (Dietary Fiber 2g)

EXCHANGES: ½ Other Carbohydrate, ½ Vegetable

CARBOHYDRATE CHOICES: ½

Carrots are a well-known source of vitamin A. Did you know that they are also a good source of fiber?

Creamy Marinated Potato Salad

START TO FINISH 30 MINUTES
12 SERVINGS (½ CUP EACH)

SALAD

1⅓ lb small red potatoes
(8 to 12 potatoes)

3 tablespoons cider vinegar

½ teaspoon salt

4 hard-cooked eggs

8 medium green onions,
  sliced (½ cup)

1 medium stalk celery, sliced
  (½ cup)

1 small red bell pepper,
  coarsely chopped

DRESSING

¾ cup fat-free mayonnaise or
  salad dressing

¼ cup fat-free sour cream

1 teaspoon sugar

2 teaspoons prepared horse-
  radish

2 teaspoons yellow mustard

¼ teaspoon coarse ground
  black pepper

1 In 4-quart saucepan or Dutch oven, place potatoes and enough water to cover. Heat to boiling. Reduce heat to medium; cook about 20 minutes or just until potatoes are fork-tender. Drain potatoes; cool slightly. Cut into 1-inch cubes. Place in large nonmetal bowl. Sprinkle with vinegar and salt; toss to coat.

2 Peel and chop eggs. Add to potatoes with remaining salad ingredients; mix gently.

3 In small bowl, mix dressing ingredients. Pour over salad; mix gently to coat. If desired, garnish with additional sliced green onions.

1 SERVING: Calories 90; Total Fat 2.5g (Saturated Fat 1g; Trans Fat 0g); Cholesterol 75mg; Sodium 270mg; Total Carbohydrate 13g (Dietary Fiber 2g)

EXCHANGES: 1 Starch, ½ Fat

CARBOHYDRATE CHOICES: 1

Prepare this potato salad a day ahead; cover and refrigerate. Just before serving, moisten with one to two tablespoons milk if dry.

Sprinkling the warm potatoes with vinegar and salt gives them a marinated quality that adds lots of flavor to this salad. The potatoes are most absorbent when warm.

Orzo-Barley Pilaf

START TO FINISH 25 MINUTES
4 SERVINGS (¾ CUP EACH)

1 can (14 oz) fat-free chicken broth with 33% less sodium

¼ cup water

½ teaspoon dried thyme leaves

¼ teaspoon salt

1 cup sliced fresh mushrooms (3 oz)

½ cup uncooked orzo or rosamarina pasta (3 oz)

½ cup uncooked quick-cooking barley

2 tablespoons sliced green onions (2 medium)

½ teaspoon grated lemon peel

Pepper to taste, if desired

1 In 2-quart nonstick saucepan, heat broth, water, thyme and salt to boiling. Stir in mushrooms, pasta and barley. Return to boiling.

2 Reduce heat to low; cover and simmer 15 to 18 minutes or until pasta and barley are tender and liquid is absorbed.

3 Stir in onions and lemon peel. Season with pepper.

1 SERVING: Calories 190; Total Fat 1g (Saturated Fat 0g; Trans Fat 0g); Cholesterol 0mg; Sodium 380mg; Total Carbohydrate 39g (Dietary Fiber 5g)

EXCHANGES: 2 Starch, 1/2 Other Carbohydrate

CARBOHYDRATE CHOICES: 2 1/2

Grain Guide

Barley The characteristic ovals, used in many hearty soups, come in whole or "pearl" forms or ground into flour. Pearl barley has the hull removed, reducing nutrition but speeding up cooking time.

Bulgur Commonly used in pilafs and salads, bulgur is wheat kernels that have been steamed, dried and crushed.

Hominy A type of corn that has been dried and hulled, hominy is available ground as grits, canned or finely ground for masa harina, the principal ingredient of corn tortillas and tamales.

Quinoa (KEEN-wah) Mild flavored and light textured, quinoa is a good source of protein. The Incas used the grain extensively; modern shoppers can find it in larger supermarkets and health food stores. It tends to be pricier than most other grains.

Wild Rice Harvested primarily in Minnesota and California, "wild rice" is actually a kind of grass. It costs more than ordinary rice, but can be blended with other rices and even a little bit will impart a nutty flavor to a dish.

Quick-cooking barley provides a convenient way to get more whole grains in your diet.

CHAPTER 3

Soups

and Sandwiches

Curried Lentil Soup

START TO FINISH 8 HOURS 20 MINUTES ▪ SLOW COOKER: 3½ TO 4 QUART

8 SERVINGS (1½ CUPS EACH)

1 bag (16 oz) dried lentils, sorted, rinsed (2½ cups)

8 cups water

2 medium carrots, cut into ½-inch slices (1 cup)

2 medium stalks celery, cut into ½-inch slices (1 cup)

1 medium onion, chopped (½ cup)

2 cloves garlic, finely chopped

2 extra-large vegetarian vegetable bouillon cubes or 2 chicken bouillon cubes

3 teaspoons curry powder

1 teaspoon salt

2 bay leaves

1 can (14.5 oz) diced tomatoes, undrained

2 cups baby or coarsely chopped fresh spinach

½ cup plain low-fat yogurt

1 In 3½- or 4-quart slow cooker, mix all ingredients except tomatoes, spinach and yogurt.

2 Cover; cook on Low heat setting 8 to 9 hours.

3 Stir in tomatoes. Cover; cook about 5 minutes longer or until hot.

4 Just before serving, discard bay leaves. Top individual servings with ¼ cup spinach and 1 tablespoon yogurt.

1 SERVING: Calories 230; Total Fat 1g (Saturated Fat 0g; Trans Fat 0g); Cholesterol 0mg; Sodium 700mg; Total Carbohydrate 39g (Dietary Fiber 11g)

EXCHANGES: 2 Starch, 1 Vegetable, 1 Very Lean Meat

CARBOHYDRATE CHOICES: 2½

Acidic ingredients, such as tomatoes, prevent lentils from cooking until they are tender.

Add the tomatoes after the lentils have cooked completely and are tender.

Chicken-Vegetable Chowder

START TO FINISH 8 HOURS ■ SLOW COOKER 2 TO 4 QUART

5 SERVINGS

1 lb boneless skinless chicken thighs, cut into 1-inch pieces

1 cup ready-to-eat baby-cut carrots, cut in half lengthwise

1 cup sliced fresh mushrooms

1 medium onion, chopped (1/2 cup)

½ cup water

¼ teaspoon garlic powder

⅛ teaspoon dried thyme leaves

1 can (14 oz) chicken broth

1 can (10¾ oz) condensed 98%-fat-free cream of chicken soup with 30% less sodium

½ cup milk

3 tablespoons all-purpose flour

1 box (9 oz) frozen cut broccoli (2 cups), thawed

1 In 3- to 4-quart slow cooker, mix chicken, carrots, mushrooms, onion, water, garlic powder, thyme and broth.

2 Cover; cook on Low heat setting 7 to 9 hours.

3 Skim fat from slow cooker. In small bowl, beat soup, milk and flour with wire whisk until smooth. Add soup mixture and broccoli to chicken mixture. Cover; cook about 30 minutes longer or until broccoli is tender.

1 SERVING: Calories 260; Total Fat 10g (Saturated Fat 3g; Trans Fat 0g); Cholesterol 60mg; Sodium 660mg; Total Carbohydrate 17g (Dietary Fiber 3g)

EXCHANGES: ½ Starch, ½ Other Carbohydrate, 1 Vegetable, 3 Lean Meat

CARBOHYDRATE CHOICES: 1

White Chili with Chicken

START TO FINISH 9 HOURS 15 MINUTES ▪ SLOW COOKER: 3½ TO 4 QUART
6 SERVINGS (1½ CUPS EACH)

1 lb boneless skinless chicken thighs, cut into thin bite-sized strips

1 cup dried great northern beans, sorted, rinsed

1 medium onion, chopped (½ cup)

1 clove garlic, finely chopped

2 teaspoons dried oregano leaves

½ teaspoon salt

1 can (10.75 oz) condensed cream of chicken soup

5 cups water

1 teaspoon ground cumin

¼ teaspoon red pepper sauce

1 can (4.5 oz) chopped green chiles

Sour cream, if desired

Chopped avocado, if desired

1 In 3½- to 4-quart slow cooker, mix chicken, beans, onion, garlic, oregano, salt, soup and water.

2 Cover; cook on Low heat setting 9 to 10 hours.

3 Just before serving, stir cumin, pepper sauce and chiles into chili. If desired, serve with additional pepper sauce. Serve with sour cream and chopped avocado.

1 SERVING: Calories 290; Total Fat 10g (Saturated Fat 3g; Trans Fat 0g); Cholesterol 50mg; Sodium 700mg; Total Carbohydrate 27g (Dietary Fiber 6g)

EXCHANGES: 2 Starch, 2½ Lean Meat

CARBOHYDRATE CHOICES: 2

Corn and Bean Chili

START TO FINISH 25 MINUTES
5 SERVINGS (1½ CUPS EACH)

1 lb. lean (at least 80%) ground beef

2 cans (15 oz.) spicy chili beans, undrained

1 can (14.5 oz.) diced tomatoes, undrained

1 can (11 oz.) vacuum-packed whole kernel corn, undrained

1 can (4.5 oz.) chopped green chiles

1 In 3-quart saucepan, cook ground beef over medium-high heat for 5 to 7 minutes or until thoroughly cooked, stirring frequently. Drain well; return to saucepan.

2 Add all remaining ingredients; mix well. Cook over medium heat for 10 to 15 minutes or until thoroughly heated and flavors are blended, stirring occasionally.

1 SERVING: Calories 420 (Calories from Fat 130); Total Fat 14g (Saturated Fat 5g); Cholesterol 55mg; Sodium 1,230mg; Total Carbohydrates 47g (Dietary Fiber 10g)

EXCHANGES: 3 Starch, 2 Medium-Fat Meat

CARBOHYDRATE CHOICES: 2½

For super-easy cleanup, serve this tasty chili in sturdy disposable bowls. Sprinkle each serving with shredded Cheddar cheese, and add warm rolled tortillas to complete the meal.

Greek Chicken Pita Folds

START TO FINISH 6 HOURS 15 MINUTES ▪ SLOW COOKER: 4 TO 6 QUART
4 SANDWICHES

1 medium onion, halved, sliced

1 clove garlic, finely chopped

1 lb boneless skinless chicken thighs

1½ teaspoons lemon-pepper seasoning

½ teaspoon dried oregano leaves

¼ teaspoon ground allspice

4 pita (pocket) breads

½ cup plain yogurt

1 plum (Roma) tomato, sliced

½ medium cucumber, chopped (about ½ cup)

1 In 4- to 6-quart slow cooker, mix onion, garlic, chicken thighs, lemon-pepper seasoning, oregano and allspice; mix to coat chicken with seasoning.

2 Cover; cook on Low heat setting 6 to 8 hours.

3 Heat pita breads as directed on package. Meanwhile, remove chicken from slow cooker; place on cutting board. Shred chicken with 2 forks.

4 To serve, stir yogurt into onion mixture in slow cooker. Spoon chicken onto warm pita breads. With slotted spoon, transfer onion mixture onto chicken; top with tomato and cucumber. Fold each pita bread in half.

1 SANDWICH: Calories 340; Total Fat 10g (Saturated Fat 3g; Trans Fat 0g); Cholesterol 75mg; Sodium 460mg; Total Carbohydrate 32g (Dietary Fiber 2g)

EXCHANGES: 1 Starch, 1 Other Carbohydrate, 4 Very Lean Meat, 1½ Fat

CARBOHYDRATE CHOICES: 2

If you don't have lemon-pepper seasoning, substitute ¾ teaspoon salt, ¼ teaspoon pepper and one teaspoon grated lemon peel.

Chicken-Bacon-Ranch Wraps

START TO FINISH 15 MINUTES
8 WRAPS

2½ cups coarsely shredded deli rotisserie chicken (from 2- to 2½-lb chicken)

1 cup shredded Monterey Jack cheese (4 oz)

4 slices cooked bacon, chopped (about ¼ cup)

¼ cup chopped green onions (4 medium)

1 cup fat-free ranch dressing

1 package (11.5 oz) flour tortillas for burritos (8 inch)

4 cups shredded romaine lettuce

1 In large bowl, gently mix all ingredients except tortillas and lettuce. Cover; refrigerate up to 3 days.

2 To make 1 wrap, in small microwavable bowl, microwave generous ⅓ cup chicken mixture, loosely covered, on High 30 to 45 seconds or until hot. Spread chicken mixture on tortilla and top with ½ cup shredded lettuce; roll up.

1 WRAP: Calories 340; Total Fat 13g (Saturated Fat 5g; Trans Fat 1g); Cholesterol 55mg; Sodium 910mg; Total Carbohydrate 33g (Dietary Fiber 1g)

EXCHANGES: 1 Starch, 1 Other Carbohydrate, 2½ Medium-Fat Meat

CARBOHYDRATE CHOICES: 2

These tasty wraps can also be served cold. For a change of flavor, why not try Cheddar cheese and iceberg lettuce instead of the Monterey Jack and romaine.

Chicken Wraps

Chicken-Apple Burgers

START TO FINISH 25 MINUTES
4 SANDWICHES

1 medium apple, finely chopped (1 cup)

4 medium green onions, finely chopped (¼ cup)

1¼ teaspoons poultry seasoning

½ teaspoon salt

2 tablespoons apple juice or water

1 lb. ground chicken or turkey

4 teaspoons honey mustard

4 burger buns, split

4 leaves leaf lettuce

1 Heat gas or charcoal grill. In medium bowl, combine apple, onions, poultry seasoning, salt and apple juice; mix well. Add ground chicken; mix well. Shape mixture into 4 (½-inch-thick) patties.

2 When grill is heated, carefully oil grill rack. Place patties on gas grill over medium heat or on charcoal grill 4 to 6 inches from medium coals. Cook covered 14 to 20 minutes or until a thermometer inserted in center of patty reads 165°F, turning patties once.

3 Spread honey mustard on bottom halves of buns. Top each with lettuce, chicken patty and top half of bun. If desired, serve with additional honey mustard.

Broiled Chicken-Apple Burgers: Place patties on oiled broiler pan; broil 4 to 6 inches from heat using times above as a guide, turning once.

1 SANDWICH: Calories 360; Total Fat 14g (Saturated Fat 4g); Cholesterol 75mg; Sodium 640mg; Total Carbohydrates 31g (Dietary Fiber 2g)

EXCHANGES: 1½ Starch, 3 Medium-Fat Meat, ½ Other Carbohydrate

CARBOHYDRATE CHOICES: 2

Planning ahead? Make up the chicken patties early in the day, and stack between pieces of waxed paper. Store in the refrigerator until dinnertime, then grill as directed in the recipe.

Georgia-Style Barbecued Turkey Sandwiches

START TO FINISH 8 HOURS 15 MINUTES ▪ SLOW COOKER: 4 TO 6 QUART
12 SANDWICHES

4 turkey thighs (about 3 lb), skin removed

½ cup packed brown sugar

¼ cup yellow mustard

2 tablespoons ketchup

2 tablespoons cider vinegar

2 tablespoons Louisiana-style hot pepper sauce

1 teaspoon salt

1 teaspoon coarse ground black pepper

1 teaspoon crushed red pepper flakes

2 teaspoons liquid smoke

12 burger buns, split

½ pint (1 cup) creamy coleslaw (from deli)

1 Spray 4- to 6-quart slow cooker with cooking spray. In slow cooker, place turkey thighs. In small bowl, mix remaining ingredients except buns and coleslaw. Pour over turkey, turning turkey as necessary to coat.

2 Cover; cook on Low heat setting 8 to 10 hours.

3 Remove turkey from slow cooker; place on cutting board. Remove meat from bones; discard bones. Shred turkey with 2 forks; return to slow cooker and mix well.

4 To serve, with slotted spoon, spoon about ⅓ cup turkey mixture onto bottom halves of buns. Top each with rounded tablespoon coleslaw. Cover with top halves of buns.

1 SANDWICH: Calories 340; Total Fat 9g (Saturated Fat 2.5g; Trans Fat 0g); Cholesterol 105mg; Sodium 610mg; Total Carbohydrate 33g (Dietary Fiber 1g)

EXCHANGES: 1½ Starch, ½ Other Carbohydrate, 3½ Very Lean Meat, 1½ Fat

CARBOHYDRATE CHOICES: 2

For a real southern treat, serve this barbecued turkey over warm baking powder biscuits. Just pop some refrigerated baking powder biscuits into the oven while you shred the turkey.

Chicken Caesar Pitas

START TO FINISH: 1 HOUR
4 SERVINGS

2 boneless skinless chicken breasts (about 4 oz each)

⅓ cup reduced-fat Caesar dressing

⅛ teaspoon pepper

2 cups coarsely chopped romaine lettuce

¼ cup shredded carrot (1 small carrot)

2 tablespoons shredded Parmesan cheese

2 whole wheat pita (pocket) breads (6 inch), cut in half to form pockets

1 plum (Roma) tomato, thinly sliced

1 Set oven control to broil. Brush both sides of chicken with 1 tablespoon of the dressing; sprinkle with pepper.

2 Place chicken on rack in broiler pan. Broil with tops 4 to 6 inches from heat 12 to 15 minutes, turning once, until juice of chicken is clear when center of thickest part is cut (170°F). Cool about 5 minutes. Cut into thin slices.

3 In medium bowl, toss lettuce, carrot and cheese with remaining dressing until coated. Fill each pita bread half with tomato and chicken; top with lettuce mixture.

1 SERVING: Calories 220; Total Fat 7g (Saturated Fat 2g; Trans Fat 0g); Cholesterol 45mg; Sodium 480mg; Total Carbohydrate 22g (Dietary Fiber 3g)

EXCHANGES: 1 Starch, ½ Vegetable, 2 Lean Meat

CARBOHYDRATE CHOICES: 1½

Hearty Meatball Sandwiches

START TO FINISH 25 MINUTES
6 SANDWICHES

¾ lb. extra-lean (at least 90%) ground beef

1 box (9 oz.) frozen spinach in a pouch, thawed, squeezed and patted dry with paper towels

1 slice whole wheat bread, torn into small pieces

½ teaspoon onion powder

1 teaspoon Italian seasoning or ½ teaspoon dried oregano leaves

1 egg or 2 egg whites

2 cups reduced-fat tomato pasta sauce

1 loaf (8 oz.) French or Italian bread

½ cup shredded mozzarella cheese (2 oz.)

2 tablespoons grated Parmesan cheese

1 Heat oven to 425°F. Line 15x10x1-inch pan with foil, extending foil over short sides of pan.

2 In medium bowl, mix ground beef, spinach, bread crumbs, onion powder, Italian seasoning and egg. Press mixture into 8×6-inch rectangle in pan. Cut rectangle into 36 pieces; do not separate.

3 Bake 10 to 15 minutes or until centers of meatballs are firm and no longer pink and juice is clear. Drain; pat beef with paper towels to remove moisture. With sharp knife, cut into 36 meatballs.

4 Meanwhile, in 3-quart saucepan, heat pasta sauce. Add meatballs; stir to coat.

5 Cut loaf of bread lengthwise to but not through one long side; cut loaf into 6 sections. Place opened sections on individual plates. Spoon 6 meatballs with sauce onto each bread section. Sprinkle with mozzarella and Parmesan cheese. Serve immediately.

1 SANDWICH: Calories 340; Total Fat 12g (Saturated Fat 4.5g; Trans Fat 0.5g); Cholesterol 80mg; Sodium 800mg; Total Carbohydrate 39g (Dietary Fiber 3g; Sugars 7g)

EXCHANGES: 2 Starch, ½ Other Carbohydrate, 2 Medium-Fat Meat, 1 Fat

CARBOHYDRATE CHOICES: 2½

Open-Faced Italian Steak Sandwiches

START TO FINISH 15 MINUTES
4 SANDWICHES

2 tablespoons butter or
    margarine, softened

1 tablespoon basil pesto

1 tablespoon sun-dried
    tomato spread

1 (1-lb.) boneless beef sirloin
    steak (about ½ inch thick),
    cut into 4 pieces

Dash salt and pepper

4 slices frozen garlic Texas
    toast

1 Heat gas or charcoal grill. In small bowl, combine butter, pesto and tomato spread; blend well. Set aside.

2 When grill is heated, sprinkle steaks with salt and pepper; place steaks on gas grill over medium heat or on charcoal grill 4 to 6 inches from medium coals. Cook covered 5 to 8 minutes or until of desired doneness, turning once.

3 During last 3 minutes of cooking time, place Texas toast on grill; cook until golden brown, turning once.

4 Place Texas toast slices on individual serving plates. Top each with 1 steak and seasoned butter.

Broiled Open-Faced Italian Steak Sandwiches: Place steaks on broiler pan; broil 4 to 6 inches from heat using times above as a guide, turning once. During last 3 minutes of cooking time, place Texas toast on broiler pan; broil until golden brown, turning once.

1 SANDWICH: Calories 330; Total Fat 17g (Saturated Fat 6g); Cholesterol 75mg; Sodium 410mg; Total Carbohydrates 18g (Dietary Fiber 1g)

EXCHANGES: 1 Starch, 3½ Lean Meat, 1½ Fat

CARBOHYDRATE CHOICES: 1

Get rid of the grit on the grill rack quickly. Just heat the rack on the grill prior to cooking, then brush the hot rack (while it's in place) with a wire grill brush or a wad of crumpled aluminum foil, and voilà, it's clean!

Beef and Cabbage Wraps

START TO FINISH 15 MINUTES
6 WRAPS

¾ lb. beef sirloin strips for stir-fry

1 medium sweet onion, chopped

3 cups coleslaw mix (shredded cabbage and carrots)

⅓ cup barbecue sauce

6 flour tortillas (8 to 10 inch), heated

1 Heat 10-inch nonstick skillet over medium-high heat. Add beef and onion; cook 3 minutes, stirring frequently, until browned.

2 Reduce heat to medium. Gently stir in coleslaw mix. Cover; cook about 2 minutes, stirring once, until cabbage is slightly wilted. Remove from heat. Stir in barbecue sauce.

3 Spoon mixture evenly onto center of each warm tortilla. To roll each, fold 1 end of tortilla up over filling; fold right and left sides over folded end, overlapping edges. Roll up tightly. Wrap each wrap securely with foil; take with you for an on-the-go dinner.

1 WRAP: Calories 230; Total Fat 5g (Saturated Fat 1.5g; Trans Fat 0.5g); Cholesterol 30mg; Sodium 370mg; Total Carbohydrate 33g (Dietary Fiber 2g; Sugars 6g)

EXCHANGES: 2 Starch, 1 Vegetable, 1 Lean Meat

CARBOHYDRATE CHOICES: 2

Italian Beef Dippers

START TO FINISH: 1 HOUR

6 SERVINGS (1 SANDWICH AND ⅓ CUP SOUP EACH)

1 can (18.5 oz) ready-to-serve French onion soup

½ teaspoon Italian seasoning

¾ lb thinly sliced cooked roast beef

6 crusty French rolls (each 3 to 4 inches long)

6 slices (½ oz each) provolone cheese

1 In 2-quart saucepan, heat soup and Italian seasoning over medium heat, stirring occasionally, until hot. Add beef. Heat 4 to 6 minutes, stirring occasionally, until hot.

2 Using serrated knife, cut rolls in half lengthwise. Remove beef from soup. Arrange beef on bottom halves of rolls.

3 Cut each slice of cheese into 2 pieces. Put 2 pieces of cheese on top of beef on each sandwich. Cover with top halves of rolls.

4 Divide soup evenly among 6 soup bowls. Serve sandwiches with warm soup for dipping.

1 SERVING: Calories 260; Total Fat 7g (Saturated Fat 3.5g; Trans Fat 0g); Cholesterol 40mg; Sodium 1320mg; Total Carbohydrate 30g (Dietary Fiber 1g)

EXCHANGES: 2 Starch, 2 Lean Meat

CARBOHYDRATE CHOICES: 2

CHAPTER 4

One-Dish
Dinners

Couscous-Stuffed Red Bell Peppers

START TO FINISH 20 MINUTES
2 SERVINGS (2 PEPPER HALVES EACH)

1 box (5.7 oz) roasted garlic and olive oil-flavored couscous mix

1¼ cups water

2 large red bell peppers, cut in half lengthwise, seeds and membranes removed

1 cup chopped fresh spinach

¼ cup grated Parmesan cheese

1 Cook couscous in water as directed on box, omitting oil; cover to keep warm.

2 Meanwhile, in 8-inch square (2-quart) microwavable dish, arrange bell pepper halves; add 2 tablespoons water. Cover with microwavable waxed paper. Microwave on High 3 to 4 minutes or just until crisp-tender.

3 Stir spinach and cheese into couscous. Spoon mixture into pepper halves.

1 SERVING: Calories 400; Total Fat 6g (Saturated Fat 2.5g; Trans Fat 0g); Cholesterol 10mg; Sodium 1030mg; Total Carbohydrate 70g (Dietary Fiber 6g)

EXCHANGES: 4 Starch, 2 Vegetable, ½ Fat

CARBOHYDRATE CHOICES: 4½

About couscous: Couscous resembles a grain but is actually a tiny pasta that's very popular in Middle Eastern cooking. Its mild flavor makes it a good complement to a variety of savory dishes, and the quick-cooking version found in most supermarkets takes only five minutes to prepare.

Looking for quick and easy recipes served in a different way? No need to precook the peppers in this recipe!

Tomato and Cheese Pasta Skillet

START TO FINISH 30 MINUTES
4 SERVINGS (1 CUP EACH)

1 can (15 oz.) Italian-style tomato sauce

1¾ cups water

1 package (7 oz.) small pasta shells (2 cups)

2 tablespoons finely chopped onion

¾ cup shredded mozzarella cheese (3 oz.)

1 In 8-inch skillet, mix tomato sauce, water, pasta and onion. Heat to boiling. Reduce heat to medium-low; cover and simmer 12 minutes, stirring occasionally.

2 Sprinkle cheese over top. Cover; cook 1 minute longer or until cheese is melted.

1 SERVING: Calories 360; Total Fat 9g (Saturated Fat 3.5g; Trans Fat 0g); Cholesterol 10mg; Sodium 640mg; Total Carbohydrate 60g (Dietary Fiber 4g, Sugars 9g)

EXCHANGES: 4 Starch, 1 Fat

CARBOHYDRATE CHOICES: 4

Foot-Long Pizza

START TO FINISH 30 MINUTES
4 SERVINGS

1 loaf (12 inch) French bread, cut in half lengthwise

¼ cup garlic-and-herbs spreadable cheese (from 4- to 6.5-oz container)

1 cup thinly sliced mushrooms

1 cup thin strips red, green or yellow bell pepper

½ cup julienne (matchstick-cut) zucchini (2x¼x¼ inch)

⅓ cup sliced ripe olives

Olive oil cooking spray or regular cooking spray

1 teaspoon Italian seasoning

½ cup shredded reduced-fat mozzarella cheese (2 oz)

1 Heat oven to 450°F. Line 15x10x1-inch pan with foil. Place bread halves, cut side up, in pan.

2 Spread spreadable cheese evenly over each bread half. Arrange mushrooms, bell pepper, zucchini and olives evenly over top. Spray gently with cooking spray. Sprinkle with Italian seasoning.

3 Bake about 15 minutes or just until vegetables begin to brown. Reduce oven temperature to 425°F. Sprinkle cheese over pizza.

4 Bake at 425°F about 5 minutes longer or until cheese is melted. Cut each bread half in half crosswise. Wrap each serving securely with foil; take with you for an on-the-go dinner.

1 SERVING: Calories 330; Total Fat 12g (Saturated Fat 6g; Trans Fat 0g); Cholesterol 25mg; Sodium 640mg; Total Carbohydrate 38g (Dietary Fiber 2g)

EXCHANGES: 2 Starch, ½ Other Carbohydrate, 1½ Lean Meat, 1½ Fat

CARBOHYDRATE CHOICES: 2½

Leek Quiche

START TO FINISH 1 HOUR 15 MINUTES
6 SERVINGS

CRUST

1 Pillsbury refrigerated pie
  crust (from 15-oz box),
  softened as directed
  on box

FILLING

2 medium leeks

2 tablespoons butter or
  margarine

3 eggs

1 cup milk

1 cup shredded Swiss cheese
  (4 oz)

½ teaspoon salt

¼ teaspoon pepper

⅛ teaspoon ground nutmeg

1 Heat oven to 400°F. Place pie crust in 9-inch glass pie plate as directed on box for One-Crust Filled Pie. Bake about 8 minutes or until very lightly browned.

2 Meanwhile, wash leeks; remove any tough outer leaves. Trim roots from white bulb portion. Cut leeks lengthwise and wash well. Cut crosswise into ½-inch-thick slices to make about 4 cups; set aside.

3 In 12-inch skillet, melt butter over medium heat. Add leeks; cook 7 to 9 minutes, stirring frequently, until tender but not brown. Remove from heat; set aside.

4 In small bowl, beat eggs with whisk. Stir in remaining filling ingredients until blended. Stir in cooked leeks. Pour mixture into partially baked crust.

5 Bake quiche 10 minutes. Cover crust edge with foil to prevent excessive browning. Reduce oven temperature to 300°F. Bake 20 to 25 minutes or until knife inserted in center comes out clean. Cool 15 minutes before serving.

1 SERVING: Calories 340; Total Fat 22g (Saturated Fat 10g; Trans Fat 1g); Cholesterol 140mg; Sodium 470mg; Total Carbohydrate 24g (Dietary Fiber 0g)

EXCHANGES: 1½ Starch, 1 High-Fat Meat, 2½ Fat

CARBOHYDRATE CHOICES: 1½

Leeks look like giant green onions and are related to both onions and garlic. Choose leeks that are firm and bright colored with an unblemished white bulb portion. Smaller leeks will be more tender than larger ones. Be sure to wash leeks thoroughly because there is often sand between the layers.

Cajun Chicken Salad

START TO FINISH 20 MINUTES
4 SERVINGS (1½ CUPS EACH)

DRESSING

2 tablespoons cider vinegar

2 to 3 teaspoons dried Cajun seasoning

⅓ cup vegetable oil

SALAD

1 package (9 oz.) frozen diced cooked chicken breast, thawed

2 cups cold cooked rice

3 stalks celery, diced (1 cup)

6 medium green onions, chopped (⅓ cup)

1 large tomato, diced (1 cup)

1 medium green bell pepper, diced (1 cup)

1 In large bowl, combine vinegar and Cajun seasoning; mix well with wire whisk. Gradually beat in oil until well blended.

2 Add salad ingredients; toss to coat. Serve immediately, or cover and refrigerate until serving time.

1 SERVING: Calories 485; Total Fat 22g (Saturated Fat 4g); Cholesterol 55mg; Sodium 300mg; Total Carbohydrates 47g (Dietary Fiber 2g)

EXCHANGES: 3 Starch, 2½ Very Lean Meat, 4 Fat

CARBOHYDRATE CHOICES: 3

With a little planning ahead you can have cooked rice in the refrigerator ready to go. When you are cooking rice, add an extra cup of uncooked rice to the pot so you have 2 cups of leftover rice. Or, stop at an Asian restaurant and buy 2 cups of cooked rice.

Beef Fried Rice

START TO FINISH: 1 HOUR
6 SERVINGS (1 ⅓ CUPS EACH)

1 cup uncooked regular long-grain white rice

2 cups water

1 teaspoon olive oil

1 egg, beaten

1 lb extra-lean (at least 90%) ground beef

1 cup sliced fresh mushrooms

½ cup sliced celery

⅓ cup reduced-sodium soy sauce

2 teaspoons sesame oil

½ teaspoon red pepper sauce

1½ cups fresh snow pea pods, cut diagonally in half

8 medium green onions, chopped (½ cup)

1 Cook rice in water as directed on package.

2 Meanwhile, brush 12-inch nonstick skillet with olive oil. Heat over medium heat. Add beaten egg to skillet; cook 1 minute or until firm but still moist. Remove from skillet; cut into thin strips. Cover to keep warm.

3 In same skillet, cook beef, mushrooms and celery over medium heat 8 to 10 minutes, stirring frequently, until beef is thoroughly cooked.

4 In small bowl, mix soy sauce, sesame oil and pepper sauce; stir into beef mixture. Add pea pods, onions, cooked egg and cooked rice; cook 2 to 3 minutes longer, stirring constantly, until hot.

1 SERVING: Calories 290; Total Fat 10g (Saturated Fat 3g; Trans Fat 0g); Cholesterol 80mg; Sodium 530mg; Total Carbohydrate 30g (Dietary Fiber 1g)

EXCHANGES: 2 Starch, 2 Lean Meat, 1/2 Fat

CARBOHYDRATE CHOICES: 2

Light-colored sesame oil adds a delicate nutty flavor to salad dressings, sautés or stir-fries. Dark sesame oil has a rich aroma that makes it perfect for flavoring finished recipes. Use either light or dark sesame oil in this fried rice.

Chicken Puttanesca Sauté

START TO FINISH 20 MINUTES
4 SERVINGS

8 oz. uncooked capellini (angel hair) pasta

1 lb. chicken breast tenders

¼ teaspoon salt

⅛ teaspoon pepper

1 tablespoon olive oil

1 can (14.5 oz.) diced tomatoes with roasted garlic, undrained

½ cup sliced green olives

⅛ teaspoon crushed red pepper flakes

1 can (14.5 oz.) cut wax or green beans, drained

1 Cook pasta as directed on package. Drain well; cover to keep warm.

2 Meanwhile, pat chicken tenders dry with paper towels; sprinkle with salt and pepper. In 10-inch nonstick skillet, heat oil over medium-high heat until hot. Add chicken; cook 4 to 6 minutes or until lightly brown on both sides.

3 Add tomatoes, olives and pepper flakes; cook 4 to 6 minutes or until chicken is no longer pink in center and liquid has been reduced slightly. Add beans; cook an additional 2 to 3 minutes or until beans are thoroughly heated.

4 Serve chicken mixture over cooked angel hair pasta.

1 SERVING: Calories 450; Total Fat 10g (Saturated Fat 2g); Cholesterol 70mg; Sodium 1,250mg; Total Carbohydrates 55g (Dietary Fiber 4g)

EXCHANGES: 3 Starch, 2 Vegetable, 3 Very Lean Meat, 1½ Fat

CARBOHYDRATE CHOICES: 0

If you don't have a can of diced tomatoes with roasted garlic, use a can of diced tomatoes and add ¼ teaspoon garlic powder.

Classic Chicken Pot Pie

START TO FINISH 1 HOUR 25 MINUTES
6 SERVINGS

CRUST

1 box (15 oz) Pillsbury refrigerated pie crusts, softened as directed on box

FILLING

⅓ cup butter or margarine

⅓ cup chopped onion

⅓ cup all-purpose flour

½ teaspoon salt

¼ teaspoon pepper

1 can (14 oz) chicken broth

½ cup milk

2½ cups shredded cooked chicken or turkey

2 cups frozen mixed vegetables, thawed

1 Heat oven to 425°F. Make pie crusts as directed on box for Two-Crust Pie, using 9-inch glass pie plate.

2 In 2-quart saucepan, melt butter over medium heat. Add onion; cook and stir about 2 minutes or until tender. Stir in flour, salt and pepper until well blended. Cook 2 to 3 minutes, stirring constantly. Gradually stir in broth and milk, cooking and stirring until bubbly and thickened. Stir in chicken and thawed mixed vegetables. Remove from heat. Spoon chicken mixture into crust-lined pie plate.

3 Cut second crust into strips. Place 5 to 7 strips across filling. Place cross-strips over tops of first strips. Seal edge and flute. Cover crust edge with foil to prevent excessive browning; remove foil during last 15 minutes of baking.

4 Bake 30 to 40 minutes or until crust is golden brown. Let stand 15 to 20 minutes before serving.

1 SERVING: Calories 600; Total Fat 34g (Saturated Fat 13g; Trans Fat 1g); Cholesterol 90mg; Sodium 940mg; Total Carbohydrate 50g (Dietary Fiber 4g)

EXCHANGES: 3½ Starch, 2 Lean Meat, 5 Fat

CARBOHYDRATE CHOICES: 3

Other frozen thawed vegetables can be used for the mixed vegetables. Try 2 cups of frozen, thawed, peas, corn or green beans.

Chicken, Mushroom and Asparagus Stir-Fry

START TO FINISH 20 MINUTES
4 SERVINGS

1 cup uncooked instant white rice

1 cup water

2 tablespoons vegetable oil

1 lb. chicken breast strips for stir-frying

1 lb. fresh asparagus spears, trimmed, cut into 2-inch pieces

1 medium onion, cut into ½-inch wedges

1 package (8 oz.) sliced fresh mushrooms (3 cups)

¼ cup water

½ cup stir-fry sauce

¼ cup oyster sauce

1 Cook rice in 1 cup water as directed on package.

2 Meanwhile, heat 1 tablespoon of the oil in wok or 10-inch skillet over medium-high heat until hot. Add chicken strips; cook and stir 5 to 6 minutes or until no longer pink in center. Remove chicken from wok; place on plate.

3 Add remaining tablespoon oil to wok. Add asparagus and onion; cook and stir 3 minutes. Add mushrooms; cook and stir an additional 3 minutes.

4 Add reserved chicken, ¼ cup water, the stir-fry sauce and oyster sauce; cover and steam 2 to 3 minutes or until asparagus is tender and chicken is hot.

1 SERVING: Calories 460; Total Fat 11g (Saturated Fat 2g); Cholesterol 70mg; Sodium 1,890mg; Total Carbohydrates 55g (Dietary Fiber 2g)

EXCHANGES: 3 Starch, 1 Vegetable, 3½ Very Lean Meat, 2 Fat

CARBOHYDRATE CHOICES: 3½

Out of oyster sauce? Use ¾ cup of the stir-fry sauce instead. Both oyster sauce and stir-fry sauce are found in the Asian foods section of the supermarket.

Sausage Veggie Hash

START TO FINISH 25 MINUTES
4 SERVINGS

1 tablespoon butter or margarine

1 cup frozen bell pepper and onion stir-fry (from 1-lb. bag)

1 bag (1 lb. 4 oz.) refrigerated new potato wedges

¼ teaspoon pepper

6 oz. cooked, smoked turkey kielbasa or Polish sausage, cut into ¼-inch slices

1½ cups frozen broccoli florets (from 14-oz. bag)

1½ cups frozen cauliflower florets (from 1-lb. bag)

½ cup shredded Cheddar and American cheese blend (2 oz.)

1 In 10-inch nonstick skillet, melt butter over medium heat. Add bell pepper and onion stir-fry, potatoes and pepper; cook 10 minutes, stirring occasionally.

2 Add kielbasa, broccoli and cauliflower; mix well. Cover; cook 8 to 10 minutes or until vegetables are tender, stirring occasionally. Remove from heat. Sprinkle with cheese; cover and let stand 1 to 2 minutes or until cheese is melted.

1 SERVING: Calories 290; Total Fat 12g (Saturated Fat 6g); Cholesterol 45mg; Sodium 960mg; Total Carbohydrates 32g (Dietary Fiber 6g)

EXCHANGES: 1½ Starch, 1 Vegetable, 1 Medium-Fat Meat, 1½ Fat

CARBOHYDRATE CHOICES: 2

Serve the finished meal right from the skillet. Just place it on a hot pad in the center of the table and add a serving spoon. There will be no serving dish to wash!

Mexican Pasta Skillet

START TO FINISH: 1 HOUR
6 SERVINGS (1⅓ CUPS EACH)

1 lb extra-lean (at least 90%) ground beef

1 jar (16 oz) mild chunky-style salsa

1 can (8 oz) tomato sauce

1½ cups water

2 cups uncooked regular or multigrain elbow macaroni

1 cup frozen corn

½ cup shredded reduced-fat sharp Cheddar cheese (2 oz)

1 In 12-inch skillet, cook beef over medium-high heat 5 to 7 minutes, stirring occasionally, until thoroughly cooked; drain.

2 Stir in salsa, tomato sauce and water. Heat to boiling. Stir in macaroni and corn. Reduce heat; cover and simmer 12 to 15 minutes, stirring occasionally, until macaroni is tender.

3 Sprinkle with cheese. Cover; let stand 1 to 2 minutes or until cheese is melted.

1 SERVING: Calories 370; Total Fat 6g (Saturated Fat 2.5g; Trans Fat 0g); Cholesterol 45mg; Sodium 650mg; Total Carbohydrate 53g (Dietary Fiber 3g)

EXCHANGES: 3½ Starch, 2 Lean Meat

CARBOHYDRATE CHOICES: 3½

Empanada Grande

START TO FINISH 45 MINUTES
3 SERVINGS

CRUST

1 Pillsbury refrigerated pie
crust (from 15-oz box),
softened as directed
on box

FILLING

1 egg

4 oz smoked chorizo sausage
links or kielbasa, casing
removed, coarsely chopped
(about 1 cup)

¾ cup frozen shredded hash
brown potatoes (from
30-oz bag), thawed

⅓ cup frozen sweet peas

1 small onion, chopped
(¼ cup)

¼ teaspoon salt

1 Heat oven to 400°F. On ungreased large cookie sheet, unroll
pie crust.

2 In large bowl, beat egg thoroughly with whisk. Reserve 1 tablespoon
egg in small bowl. Stir remaining filling ingredients into egg in
large bowl.

3 Spoon filling mixture evenly onto half of crust to within ½ inch of
edge. Brush edge of crust with reserved 1 tablespoon beaten egg. Fold
crust over filling; press edges with fork to seal. Cut several slits in top
of crust. Brush top with remaining beaten egg.

4 Bake 25 to 30 minutes or until golden brown. Cut into wedges.

1 SERVING: Calories 560; Total Fat 35g (Saturated Fat 13g; Trans Fat 0g); Cholesterol 115mg; Sodium 1000mg;
Total Carbohydrate 49g (Dietary Fiber 2g)

EXCHANGES: 3 Starch, ½ High-Fat Meat, 6 Fat

CARBOHYDRATE CHOICES: 3

If you forgot to thaw the potatoes, you can quickly thaw them in the microwave.
Place them on a microwavable plate, and microwave uncovered on Medium for
1 minute.

Individual Pepperoni Pizzas

START TO FINISH 20 MINUTES
4 PIZZAS

4 flour tortillas (8 inch)

2 teaspoons olive oil

1½ cups finely shredded
   Cheddar and Monterey Jack
   cheese blend (6 oz.)

½ cup sliced pimiento-stuffed
   green olives

½ cup diced tomato, well
   drained

24 slices (1 inch) pepperoni

1 teaspoon dried oregano
   leaves

1 Heat gas or charcoal grill. Place tortillas on ungreased cookie sheets. Brush with oil. Sprinkle with 1 cup of the cheese. Top evenly with olives, tomato and pepperoni. Sprinkle with remaining cheese and oregano.

2 When grill is heated, with broad spatula, carefully slide pizzas onto gas grill over medium heat or onto charcoal grill 4 to 6 inches from medium coals. Cook covered 3 to 6 minutes or until cheese is melted and crust is crisp. To remove from grill, slide pizzas back onto cookie sheets.

1 PIZZA: Calories 515; Total Fat 36g (Saturated Fat 15g); Cholesterol 70mg; Sodium 1,590mg; Total Carbohydrates 27g (Dietary Fiber 1g)

EXCHANGES: 2 Starch, 2 High-Fat Meat, 4 Fat

CARBOHYDRATE CHOICES: 2

Assemble these tasty pizzas on a large rimless cookie sheet, and they will slide easily on and off the hot grill. If all of your cookie sheets have rims, simply turn one upside down and assemble the pizzas on the underside. This tricky technique not only helps transfer the pizzas easily but also keeps them conveniently all together.

Basil-Pork and Asian Noodles

START TO FINISH 25 MINUTES
4 SERVINGS

8 oz. uncooked capellini (angel hair) pasta

2 teaspoons sesame oil

1 tablespoon sesame seed

1 lb. pork tenderloin, halved lengthwise, thinly sliced

1 medium onion, cut into thin wedges

½ cup stir-fry sauce

2 tablespoons honey

2 cups frozen sugar snap peas (from 1-lb. bag)

¼ cup sliced fresh basil

1 Cook pasta as directed on package. Drain; return to saucepan. Add sesame oil; toss to coat. Cover to keep warm.

2 Meanwhile, heat 10-inch nonstick skillet over medium-high heat until hot. Add sesame seed; cook and stir 2 to 3 minutes or until golden brown. (Watch carefully to prevent burning.) Remove from skillet.

3 In same skillet, cook pork and onion over medium-high heat for 3 to 4 minutes or until no longer pink, stirring frequently.

4 Add stir-fry sauce, honey and sugar snap peas; mix well. Reduce heat to medium; cook 3 to 4 minutes or until peas are crisp-tender, stirring occasionally. Add basil; cook and stir 1 minute. Serve pork mixture over cooked pasta. Sprinkle with toasted sesame seed.

1 SERVING: Calories 500; Total Fat 9g (Saturated Fat 2g); Cholesterol 70mg; Sodium 1,660mg; Total Carbohydrates 67g (Dietary Fiber 5g)

EXCHANGES: 4 Starch, 1 Vegetable, 3½ Lean Meat

CARBOHYDRATE CHOICES: 0

Speed up this meal even more by using refrigerated angel hair pasta. A 9-ounce package is just right, and it cooks in less than half the time of dried pasta.

Hamburger Hash Skillet Supper

START TO FINISH 25 MINUTES

5 SERVINGS (1⅓ CUPS EACH)

1 lb. lean (at least 80%) ground beef

1 bag (1 lb. 4 oz.) refrigerated diced potatoes with onions

½ cup chopped red onion

⅓ cup whipping cream

1 tablespoon Worcestershire sauce

1 teaspoon celery salt

¼ teaspoon pepper

2 medium tomatoes, chopped (1¼ cups)

1 In 12-inch nonstick skillet, cook ground beef, potatoes and red onion over medium heat for 10 to 15 minutes or until beef is thoroughly cooked and potatoes are tender, stirring frequently. Drain well.

2 Stir cream, Worcestershire sauce, celery salt and pepper into beef mixture; blend well. Cook an additional 2 to 5 minutes or until mixture is bubbly around edges, stirring frequently. Gently stir in tomatoes.

1 SERVING: Calories 350; Total Fat 18g (Saturated Fat 8g); Cholesterol 70mg; Sodium 660mg; Total Carbohydrates 27g (Dietary Fiber 2g)

EXCHANGES: 2 Starch, 2 Medium-Fat Meat, 1½ Fat

CARBOHYDRATE CHOICES: 2

Thaw frozen ground beef quickly in the microwave on Defrost for 4 to 6 minutes. If necessary, microwave in additional increments of 30 seconds until thawed. It helps to turn the package over once or twice while it is thawing.

Tex-Mex Meatball Pie

START TO FINISH 55 MINUTES
6 SERVINGS

CRUST

1 Pillsbury refrigerated pie crust (from 15-oz box), softened as directed on box

FILLING

18 frozen cooked meatballs (about 1 inch), thawed

1 cup frozen whole kernel corn

½ cup chunky-style salsa

¾ cup shredded Cheddar cheese (3 oz)

TOPPINGS

1 cup shredded lettuce

¼ cup sour cream

Additional chunky-style salsa or chopped tomatoes

1 Heat oven to 375°F. On ungreased cookie sheet, unroll pie crust. Place meatballs on center of crust.

2 In small bowl, mix corn and ½ cup salsa. Spoon corn mixture over meatballs. Carefully fold 2-inch edge of crust over filling, pleating crust slightly as necessary (see photo).

3 Bake 35 to 40 minutes or until crust is deep golden brown. Sprinkle with cheese. Bake 3 to 5 minutes longer or until cheese is melted.

4 Serve with lettuce, sour cream and additional salsa. Serve immediately.

1 SERVING: Calories 340; Total Fat 20g (Saturated Fat 9g; Trans Fat 0g); Cholesterol 60mg; Sodium 640mg; Total Carbohydrate 29g (Dietary Fiber 0g)

EXCHANGES: 1½ Starch, ½ Other Carbohydrate, 1 High-Fat Meat, 2 Fat

CARBOHYDRATE CHOICES: 2

If the meatballs are larger than 1 inch, cut them in half before placing on the pie crust. Taco-flavored Cheddar cheese is also great in this fun dinner pie.

Sloppy Joe Confetti Tacos

START TO FINISH 20 MINUTES

6 SERVINGS (2 TACOS EACH)

1 lb extra-lean (at least 90%) ground beef

1 box (4.6 oz) taco shells (12 shells)

1 can (15.5 oz) sloppy joe sauce

1 small red bell pepper, chopped

1 can (11 oz) whole kernel sweet corn, drained

1 can (2.75 oz) sliced ripe olives, drained

1 cup thinly sliced romaine lettuce

¼ cup shredded mozzarella cheese (1 oz)

¼ cup shredded reduced-fat sharp Cheddar cheese (1 oz)

1 Heat oven to 350°F. In 10-inch skillet, cook beef over medium-high heat 5 to 7 minutes, stirring frequently, until thoroughly cooked; drain if necessary.

2 Meanwhile, heat taco shells as directed on box.

3 Stir sloppy joe sauce, bell pepper and corn into beef. Cook 2 to 3 minutes longer, stirring occasionally, until mixture is hot and bubbly.

4 Spoon about ¼ cup beef mixture into each warm taco shell; top with olives, lettuce and cheeses.

1 SERVING: Calories 330; Total Fat 13g (Saturated Fat 4.5g; Trans Fat 1.5g); Cholesterol 50mg; Sodium 850mg; Total Carbohydrate 31g (Dietary Fiber 4g)

EXCHANGES: 1½ Starch, ½ Other Carbohydrate, 2 Medium-Fat Meat, ½ Fat

CARBOHYDRATE CHOICES: 2

Use taco shells with flat bottoms for easier filling and a little extra room.

Taco-Topped Potatoes

START TO FINISH 25 MINUTES
4 SERVINGS

4 medium baking potatoes

1 container (18 oz.) refrigerated taco sauce with seasoned ground beef

½ cup shredded Cheddar cheese (2 oz.)

1 medium Italian plum tomato, chopped (⅓ cup)

2 medium green onions, sliced (2 tablespoons)

1 Pierce potatoes with fork. Arrange in spoke pattern on microwave-safe paper towel in microwave. Microwave on High for 12 to 14 minutes or until tender, turning potatoes and rearranging halfway through cooking. Cool 3 minutes.

2 Meanwhile, heat taco sauce with seasoned ground beef as directed on container.

3 To serve, place potatoes on individual serving plates. Cut potatoes in half lengthwise; mash slightly with fork. Spoon about ½ cup ground beef mixture over each potato. Top with cheese, tomato and onions.

1 SERVING: Calories 340; Total Fat 17g (Saturated Fat 8g); Cholesterol 50mg; Sodium 770mg; Total Carbohydrates 35g (Dietary Fiber 2g)

EXCHANGES: 2 Starch, 1 Vegetable, 2 Medium-Fat Meat

CARBOHYDRATE CHOICES: 2

Look for tubs of the taco sauce with seasoned ground beef in the refrigerated meat case at the grocery store. It's a great product to have on hand for quick tacos or meals such as this. The microwavable ground beef is ready to serve in 6 minutes and can be frozen for longer storage.

Beef and Ramen Noodle Bowls

START TO FINISH 20 MINUTES
4 SERVINGS (1½ CUPS EACH)

1 tablespoon vegetable oil

1 medium onion, cut into thin wedges

1 bag (1 lb. 5 oz.) frozen stir-fry vegetables with traditional teriyaki sauce meal starter

¾ cup water

1 tablespoon peanut butter

1 package (3 oz.) oriental-flavor ramen noodle soup mix

¾ lb. cooked roast beef (from deli), cut into thin bite-size strips

¼ cup chopped peanuts

1 In 10-inch skillet, heat oil over medium-high heat until hot. Add onion; cook and stir 1 minute. Add frozen sauce from meal starter, water, peanut butter and 1 teaspoon of the seasoning from soup mix; discard remaining seasoning. Cook 2 to 3 minutes or until sauce is thawed, stirring occasionally.

2 Break up ramen noodles (from soup mix) into skillet. Add frozen vegetables; cover and cook an additional 8 to 10 minutes or until vegetables are crisp-tender, stirring occasionally.

3 Add beef; cook and stir until thoroughly heated. Spoon mixture into individual serving bowls. Sprinkle with peanuts.

1 SERVING: Calories 340; Total Fat 16g (Saturated Fat 3g); Cholesterol 40mg; Sodium 1,850mg; Total Carbohydrates 30g (Dietary Fiber 5g)

EXCHANGES: 1 Starch, 1 Vegetable, 3 Lean Meat, 1½ Fat

CARBOHYDRATE CHOICES: 0

To easily break up the ramen noodles before adding them to the skillet, gently pound the unopened package with a rolling pin or wooden spoon.

Ravioli with Corn and Cilantro 126 •

Chicken with Chipotle Avocado Salsa 128 •

Grilled Lemon-Rosemary Chicken 130 • Spicy Chinese Chicken Tacos 132 •

Balsamic-Glazed Chicken Breasts 134 •

Lemon-Basil Skillet Chicken with Rice 136 •

Asian Chicken Salad with Peanuts 138 • Turkey Meat Loaves 140 •

Chicken with Caramelized Onion Glaze 142 •

Sweet-and-Sour Pork Chops 144 •

Honey-Glazed Pork Chops 146 • Pork and Pineapple Stir-Fry 148 •

Milanese Beef Grill 150 • Beef with Burgundy Mushrooms 152 •

Crispy Oven-Baked Fish 154 • Swordfish with Pineapple Salsa 156 •

Grilled Marinated Shrimp 158 •

Salmon with Lemon Butter and Pineapple Salsa 160 •

Pan-Roasted Halibut over Rotini 162

CHAPTER 5

Quick
and Easy Meals

Ravioli with Corn and Cilantro

START TO FINISH 20 MINUTES
3 SERVINGS (1¼ CUPS EACH)

1 package (9 oz.) refrigerated roasted-chicken-and-garlic-filled or cheese-filled ravioli

2 tablespoons olive oil

2 garlic cloves, minced, or ¼ teaspoon garlic powder

1 can (11 oz.) whole kernel corn with red and green peppers, drained

¼ teaspoon salt

¼ cup chopped fresh cilantro

1 Cook ravioli as directed on package. Drain.

2 Meanwhile, in large skillet, heat oil over medium heat until hot. Add garlic; cook and stir 2 to 3 minutes or until tender. Add corn and salt; cook until thoroughly heated, stirring occasionally.

3 Add cooked ravioli; toss to coat. Sprinkle with cilantro.

1 SERVING: Calories 320; Total Fat 17g (Saturated Fat 5g); Cholesterol 85mg; Sodium 900mg; Total Carbohydrates 33g (Dietary Fiber 3g)

EXCHANGES: 2 Starch, 1 High-Fat Meat, 1½ Fat

CARBOHYDRATE CHOICES: 2

If fresh cilantro isn't available, you can use ¼ cup fresh chopped or 1 tablespoon dried basil instead.

Chicken with Chipotle-Avocado Salsa

START TO FINISH 45 MINUTES
8 SERVINGS

CHICKEN

1 package (1.25 oz) taco
   seasoning mix

2 tablespoons olive oil

2 tablespoons lime juice

1 tablespoon honey

2 quartered whole chickens
   (3 to 3½ lb each), skin and
   fat removed if desired

SALSA

1 medium tomato, chopped

1 medium avocado, pitted,
   peeled and chopped

2 tablespoons chopped fresh
   cilantro

2 tablespoons finely chopped
   red onion

½ teaspoon garlic salt

1 to 2 teaspoons chopped
   chipotle chiles in adobo
   sauce (from 7- or
   11-oz can)

1 Heat gas or charcoal grill. In medium bowl, mix taco seasoning mix, oil, lime juice and honey. Brush mixture evenly over all sides of chicken quarters.

2 Place chicken on grill over medium heat. Cook 30 to 40 minutes, turning frequently, until juice of chicken is clear when thickest piece is cut to bone (170°F for breasts; 180°F for thighs and legs).

3 Meanwhile, in medium bowl, mix all salsa ingredients. Serve salsa with chicken.

1 SERVING: Calories 320; Total Fat 16g (Saturated Fat 3.5g; Trans Fat 0g); Cholesterol 110mg; Sodium 350mg; Total Carbohydrate 8g (Dietary Fiber 2g; Sugars 5g)

EXCHANGES: ½ Other Carbohydrate, 5 Lean Meat

CARBOHYDRATE CHOICES: ½

Grilled Lemon-Rosemary Chicken

START TO FINISH 1 HOUR 50 MINUTES
8 SERVINGS

⅔ cup olive oil

¼ cup chopped fresh
  rosemary leaves

4 teaspoons grated lemon
  peel

½ teaspoon garlic salt

½ teaspoon lemon-pepper
  seasoning

⅓ cup fresh lemon juice

2 tablespoons honey

4 cloves garlic, finely chopped

4½ to 5 lb chicken pieces
  (breasts, legs, thighs)

1 In large bowl or resealable food-storage plastic bag, mix all ingredients except chicken. Add chicken; turn to coat. Cover bowl or seal bag; refrigerate at least 1 hour or up to 4 hours to marinate.

2 Heat gas or charcoal grill. Remove chicken from marinade; reserve marinade. Place chicken, skin side down, on grill over medium heat. Cook 10 minutes.

3 Brush chicken with marinade; turn chicken. Cook 20 to 30 minutes longer, turning and brushing frequently with marinade, until juice of chicken is clear when thickest piece is cut to bone (170°F for breasts; 180°F for thighs and legs). Discard any remaining marinade.

1 SERVING: Calories 360; Total Fat 23g (Saturated Fat 5g; Trans Fat 0g); Cholesterol 110mg; Sodium 140mg; Total Carbohydrate 3g (Dietary Fiber 0g; Sugars 2g)

EXCHANGES: 5 Lean Meat, 2 Fat

CARBOHYDRATE CHOICES: 0

Spicy Chinese Chicken Tacos

START TO FINISH 20 MINUTES
6 SERVINGS (2 TACOS EACH)

1 box (4.6 oz) taco shells
   (12 shells)

3 boneless skinless chicken
   breasts (¾ lb), cut into thin
   bite-size strips

1 teaspoon grated gingerroot

1 small clove garlic, finely
   chopped

2 tablespoons soy sauce

1 tablespoon honey

1 large green onion, sliced

½ teaspoon crushed red
   pepper flakes

1½ cups shredded iceberg
   lettuce

1 If desired, heat taco shells as directed on box.

2 Heat 10-inch nonstick skillet over medium-high heat. Add chicken, gingerroot and garlic; cook 3 to 5 minutes, stirring frequently, until lightly browned.

3 Stir in soy sauce, honey, onion and pepper flakes to coat. Reduce heat to low; cover and cook 5 minutes, stirring occasionally, until chicken is no longer pink in center.

4 To serve, place slightly less than ¼ cup chicken mixture in each taco shell. Top each with lettuce. Serve immediately.

1 SERVING: Calories 190; Total Fat 7g (Saturated Fat 1.5g; Trans Fat 1g); Cholesterol 35mg; Sodium 420mg; Total Carbohydrate 18g (Dietary Fiber 1g)

EXCHANGES: 1 Starch, 1½ Lean Meat, ½ Fat

CARBOHYDRATE CHOICES: 1

While a glass of water might seem ideal to douse a peppery "fire" in the mouth, a mild starch such as bread or rice or a dairy product (milk or yogurt) works better to neutralize the heat from hot chiles.

Balsamic-Glazed Chicken Breasts

START TO FINISH: 1 HOUR 5 MINUTES
4 SERVINGS

GLAZE

⅓ cup packed brown sugar

⅓ cup balsamic vinegar

1 teaspoon chopped fresh rosemary leaves

1 teaspoon finely chopped garlic

CHICKEN

4 bone-in skin-on chicken breasts (8 oz each)

½ teaspoon salt

¼ teaspoon pepper

1 Heat gas or charcoal grill. In small bowl, mix glaze ingredients; set aside.

2 Sprinkle chicken with salt and pepper. Place chicken on grill, skin side down. Cover grill; cook 10 minutes over medium heat. Turn chicken; brush half the glaze evenly over chicken. Continue cooking and brushing with remaining glaze 10 to 12 minutes longer or until juice of chicken is clear when thickest part is cut to bone (170°F).

1 SERVING: Calories 310; Total Fat 9g (Saturated Fat 2.5g; Trans Fat 0g); Cholesterol 95mg; Sodium 380mg; Total Carbohydrate 22g (Dietary Fiber 0g)

EXCHANGES: 1 Other Carbohydrate, 4 1/2 Lean Meat

CARBOHYDRATE CHOICES: 1½

Substitution Idea: Substitute any fresh herb, such as thyme, oregano, tarragon or Italian parsley, for the rosemary in this recipe.

Lemon-Basil Skillet Chicken with Rice

START TO FINISH 10 MINUTES
4 SERVINGS

4 boneless, skinless chicken breasts (1 lb.)

Paprika

1½ cups hot water

1½ cups uncooked instant white rice

2 tablespoons butter or margarine

1 tablespoon lemon juice

1 teaspoon dried basil leaves

¼ teaspoon salt

1 Heat 10-inch nonstick skillet over high heat. Sprinkle both sides of chicken breasts with paprika; add to hot skillet. Immediately reduce heat to medium-high; cover and cook 4 minutes.

2 Meanwhile, in 2-quart saucepan, place hot water; cover tightly. Heat to boiling. Stir in rice; remove from heat. Let stand 5 minutes.

3 Turn chicken; cover and cook 4 to 5 minutes longer or until juice of chicken is no longer pink when center of thickest part is cut (170°F). Remove chicken from skillet; place on serving platter. Cover to keep warm.

4 In same hot skillet, mix butter, lemon juice, basil and salt. If necessary, return to heat to melt butter.

5 Place rice on serving platter; arrange chicken over rice. Spoon butter mixture over chicken.

1 SERVING: Calories 340; Total Fat 10g (Saturated Fat 4g; Trans Fat 0g); Cholesterol 85mg; Sodium 250mg; Total Carbohydrate 35g (Dietary Fiber 0g; Sugars 0g)

EXCHANGES: 2 Starch, 3 Very Lean Meat, 1½ Fat

CARBOHYDRATE CHOICES: 2

Asian Chicken Salad with Peanuts

START TO FINISH: 40 MINUTES
4 SERVINGS

1 lb uncooked chicken breast strips for stir-frying

¾ cup Oriental dressing and marinade

2 teaspoons vegetable oil

3 cups thinly sliced Chinese (napa) cabbage

3 cups fresh baby spinach leaves

¼ cup sliced green onions (4 medium)

2 tablespoons coarsely chopped dry-roasted peanuts

Additional dressing, if desired

1 In medium bowl, mix chicken and ¼ cup of the dressing; toss to coat. Let stand at room temperature 10 minutes to marinate.

2 In 8-inch nonstick skillet, heat oil over medium-high heat until hot. Remove chicken from marinade with slotted spoon and add to skillet; discard remaining marinade. Cook and stir chicken 4 to 6 minutes or until browned and no longer pink in center. Remove from heat. Add remaining ½ cup dressing; stir to mix.

3 Divide cabbage and spinach evenly among 4 serving plates. Top with chicken mixture. Sprinkle with onions and peanuts. Serve with additional dressing.

1 SERVING: Calories 200; Total Fat 8g (Saturated Fat 2g; Trans Fat 0g); Cholesterol 70mg; Sodium 600mg; Total Carbohydrate 3g (Dietary Fiber 1g)

EXCHANGES: 1 Vegetable, 3 Lean Meat

CARBOHYDRATE CHOICES: 0

Turkey Meat Loaves

START TO FINISH 40 MINUTES
6 SERVINGS (2 LOAVES EACH)

1½ lb. ground turkey breast

¾ cup old-fashioned or quick-cooking oats

1 small red bell pepper, finely chopped

½ cup apple juice

3 teaspoons onion powder

1 teaspoon salt

1 teaspoon dried sage leaves, crushed

½ teaspoon pepper

¼ teaspoon garlic powder

2 tablespoons apple juice

1 Heat oven to 375°F. Spray 12 regular-size muffin cups with cooking spray. In medium bowl, mix all ingredients except 2 tablespoons apple juice.

2 Spoon mixture evenly into muffin cups, mounding tops. Brush tops with 2 tablespoons apple juice.

3 Bake 20 to 30 minutes or until thermometer inserted in center of loaf reads 165°F.

1 SERVING: Calories 210; Total Fat 7g (Saturated Fat 2g; Trans Fat 0g); Cholesterol 75mg; Sodium 470mg; Total Carbohydrate 12g (Dietary Fiber 1g; Sugars 4g)

EXCHANGES: ½ Starch, 3½ Very Lean Meat, 1 Fat

CARBOHYDRATE CHOICES: 1

Chicken with Caramelized Onion Glaze

START TO FINISH 40 MINUTES
4 SERVINGS

½ cup raspberry spreadable fruit

1½ teaspoons grated gingerroot

1 tablespoon red wine vinegar

1 tablespoon soy sauce

2 teaspoons canola or soybean oil

1 medium onion, chopped (½ cup)

4 bone-in chicken breasts, skin removed

1 Heat gas or charcoal grill. In small bowl, beat raspberry spreadable fruit, gingerroot, vinegar and soy sauce with wire whisk until well blended; set aside.

2 In 10-inch nonstick skillet, heat oil over high heat 1 minute. Add onion; cook and stir 2 minutes. Reduce heat to medium; cook 2 minutes longer or until onion is tender and rich dark brown. Reduce heat to low; stir in raspberry mixture. Cook 1 minute, stirring constantly. Remove from heat; set aside.

3 When grill is heated, place chicken, bone side up, on gas grill over medium-high heat or on charcoal grill over medium-high coals; cover grill. Cook 15 to 17 minutes, turning frequently, until juice of chicken is no longer pink when centers of thickest part is cut to bone (170°F). Spoon onion-raspberry mixture over meaty side of chicken; cook uncovered 2 minutes longer.

1 SERVING: Calories 270; Total Fat 7g (Saturated Fat 1.5g; Trans Fat 0g); Cholesterol 75mg; Sodium 300mg; Total Carbohydrate 26g (Dietary Fiber 3g; Sugars 21g)

EXCHANGES: 1½ Other Carbohydrate, 4 Very Lean Meat, 1 Fat

CARBOHYDRATE CHOICES: 2

Sweet-and-Sour Pork Chops

START TO FINISH 15 MINUTES
4 SERVINGS

⅓ cup honey

2 tablespoons prepared yellow mustard

⅛ teaspoon ground cloves

½ teaspoon onion salt

¼ teaspoon pepper

4 boneless pork loin chops, ¾ inch thick (1 lb.)

Orange slices, if desired

1 In small bowl, mix honey, mustard and cloves. Sprinkle onion salt and pepper over pork chops.

2 Heat 10-inch nonstick skillet over medium-high heat. Add pork chops; cook 3 minutes. Turn pork. Reduce heat to medium-low; pour honey mixture over pork chops. Cover; cook 5 to 8 minutes longer or until pork is slightly pink in center and thermometer inserted in center of pork reads 160°F. If desired, garnish with orange slices.

1 SERVING: Calories 310; Total Fat 13g (Saturated Fat 4.5g; Trans Fat 0g); Cholesterol 70mg; Sodium 330mg; Total Carbohydrate 24g (Dietary Fiber 0g; Sugars 24g)

EXCHANGES: 1½ Other Carbohydrate, 3½ Lean Meat, ½ Fat

CARBOHYDRATE CHOICES: 1½

Honey-Glazed Pork Chops

START TO FINISH 25 MINUTES
4 SERVINGS

GLAZE

2 tablespoons ketchup

2 tablespoons honey

2 tablespoons white wine vinegar

1 teaspoon dried thyme leaves

½ teaspoon ground mustard

2 garlic cloves, minced, or ¼ teaspoon garlic powder

PORK CHOPS

1 teaspoon paprika

½ teaspoon peppered sea-soned salt

4 (6- to 7-oz. each) bone-in pork loin chops

1 Heat gas or charcoal grill. In small microwavable bowl, combine all glaze ingredients; mix well. Microwave on High for 30 seconds. Stir; set aside.

2 In small bowl, combine paprika and peppered seasoned salt. Sprinkle both sides of pork chops with paprika mixture; rub into surface of pork.

3 When grill is heated, place pork on gas grill over medium heat or on charcoal grill 4 to 6 inches from medium coals. Cook covered 12 to 15 minutes or until pork is slightly pink when cut near bone, turning twice, and brushing glaze on each side during last 5 minutes of cooking time. Discard any remaining glaze.

1 SERVING: Calories 230; Total Fat 10g (Saturated Fat 4g); Cholesterol 85mg; Sodium 140mg; Total Carbohydrates 5g (Dietary Fiber 0g)

EXCHANGES: 4½ Lean Meat

CARBOHYDRATE CHOICES: 0

Broiled Honey-Glazed Pork Chops: Place pork chops on broiler pan; broil 4 to 6 inches from heat using times above as a guide, turning twice, and brushing glaze on each side during last 2 minutes of cooking time.

Avoid all of that running back and forth from the kitchen to the grill by outfitting yourself with a tool with all the essentials you're likely to need at the grill. Choose a wicker, plastic or wire basket that your tools will fit in, and keep it ready to go for grill nights!

Pork and Pineapple Stir-Fry

START TO FINISH 20 MINUTES

4 SERVINGS (1¾ CUPS EACH)

1¼ cups uncooked instant rice

1¾ cups water

4 tablespoons packed brown sugar

1½ teaspoons cornstarch

½ teaspoon ground ginger

¼ teaspoon crushed red pepper flakes, if desired

3 tablespoons soy sauce

1 can (20 oz) pineapple chunks or 16 fresh pineapple chunks, drained, 2 tablespoons liquid reserved

¾ lb boneless lean pork, cut into thin bite-size strips

1 bag (16 oz) coleslaw mix (shredded cabbage and carrots)

1 Cook rice in 1¼ cups of the water as directed on package.

2 Meanwhile, in small bowl, mix 3 tablespoons of the brown sugar, the cornstarch, ginger, pepper flakes, the remaining ½ cup water, the soy sauce and reserved 2 tablespoons pineapple liquid; set aside.

3 Heat 12-inch nonstick skillet over medium-high heat. Add drained pineapple chunks; sprinkle with remaining 1 tablespoon brown sugar. Cook 5 minutes, turning chunks occasionally.

4 Remove pineapple from skillet; set aside. In same skillet, cook and stir pork over medium-high heat 2 minutes.

5 Add coleslaw mix; cook and stir 3 to 6 minutes or until pork is no longer pink in center and cabbage is tender.

6 Stir pineapple and cornstarch mixture into pork mixture; cook and stir about 3 minutes or until pork is glazed and sauce is slightly thickened. Serve over rice.

1 SERVING: Calories 440; Total Fat 7g (Saturated Fat 2.5g; Trans Fat 0g); Cholesterol 55mg; Sodium 750mg; Total Carbohydrate 69g (Dietary Fiber 5g)

EXCHANGES: 1 Starch, 1 Fruit, 2 Other Carbohydrate, 1½ Vegetable, 2½ Lean Meat

CARBOHYDRATE CHOICES: 4½

Milanese Beef Grill

START TO FINISH 20 MINUTES
4 SERVINGS

1 lb. boneless beef top round steak (¾ inch thick)

¼ teaspoon salt

⅛ to ¼ teaspoon pepper

⅓ cup finely chopped fresh parsley

2 tablespoons grated lemon peel

3 large cloves garlic, minced

¼ cup dry white wine or chicken broth

1 tablespoon Dijon mustard

1 Heat gas or charcoal grill. Lightly sprinkle both sides of steak with salt and pepper.

2 When grill is heated, place steak on gas grill over medium heat or on charcoal grill over medium coals; cover grill. Cook 8 to 11 minutes, turning once, until desired doneness.

3 Meanwhile, in shallow dish, mix remaining ingredients.

4 Remove steak from grill; cut diagonally across grain into slices. Coat each slice with sauce mixture before placing on individual plates. Spoon any remaining sauce over steak slices.

1 SERVING: Calories 130; Total Fat 4g (Saturated Fat 1g; Trans Fat 0g); Cholesterol 60mg; Sodium 290mg; Total Carbohydrate 2g (Dietary Fiber 0g; Sugars 0g)

EXCHANGES: 3 Very Lean Meat, ½ Fat

CARBOHYDRATE CHOICES: 0

Beef with Burgundy Mushrooms

START TO FINISH 25 MINUTES
4 SERVINGS

2 cups uncooked medium egg noodles (4 oz)

1 lb boneless beef sirloin steak (½ inch thick), cut into 4 pieces

2 packages (8 oz each) fresh whole mushrooms, quartered

1 can (10½ oz) condensed French onion soup

¼ cup dry red wine (such as Burgundy) or nonalcoholic wine

1 tablespoon cornstarch

3 tablespoons tomato paste with basil, garlic and oregano

½ teaspoon dried oregano leaves

2 tablespoons chopped fresh parsley

Pepper

1 Cook and drain noodles as directed on package, omitting salt. Place in serving bowl; cover to keep warm.

2 Meanwhile, heat 12-inch nonstick skillet over medium-high heat. Add beef; cook 3 to 4 minutes on each side or until desired doneness. Remove from heat. Place beef on serving platter; cover to keep warm.

3 Wipe skillet clean with paper towels. Heat skillet again over medium-high heat. Add mushrooms; cook 10 minutes, stirring occasionally.

4 Meanwhile, in medium bowl, mix soup, wine, cornstarch, tomato paste and oregano.

5 Add soup mixture to mushrooms; cook, stirring frequently, until bubbly and thickened. Remove from heat. Stir in parsley, and season to taste with pepper. Spoon mushroom mixture over beef; serve with noodles.

1 SERVING: Calories 350; Total Fat 8g (Saturated Fat 2g; Trans Fat 0g); Cholesterol 95mg; Sodium 720mg; Total Carbohydrate 32g (Dietary Fiber 3g)

EXCHANGES: 1½ Starch, ½ Other Carbohydrate, 4½ Very Lean Meat, 1 Fat

CARBOHYDRATE CHOICES: 2

Crispy Oven-Baked Fish

START TO FINISH 30 MINUTES
2 SERVINGS

1 egg or 1 egg white

1 teaspoon water

⅓ cup Italian-style dry bread crumbs

½ teaspoon lemon-pepper seasoning

¼ teaspoon garlic salt

2 catfish or tilapia fillets (3 to 4 oz. each)

Cooking spray

4 lemon wedges

1 Heat oven to 400°F. Line cookie sheet with foil; generously spray foil with cooking spray. In shallow bowl or dish, beat egg and water with wire whisk until well blended. In another shallow bowl or dish, mix bread crumbs, lemon-pepper seasoning and garlic salt.

2 Dip fish into egg mixture; coat with bread crumb mixture. Place on cookie sheet. Spray fish with cooking spray.

3 Bake 10 minutes. Turn fillets; bake 5 to 10 minutes longer or until fish flakes easily with fork. Place fillets on serving platter; garnish with lemon wedges.

1 SERVING: Calories 280; Total Fat 12g (Saturated Fat 2.5g; Trans Fat 0g); Cholesterol 190mg; Sodium 460mg; Total Carbohydrate 15g (Dietary Fiber 0g; Sugars 2g)

EXCHANGES: 1 Starch, 4 Lean Meat

CARBOHYDRATE CHOICES: 1

Swordfish with Pineapple Salsa

START TO FINISH 25 MINUTES
6 SERVINGS

SALSA

½ medium fresh pineapple, rind removed, cored and finely chopped

1 red bell pepper, seeded, finely chopped

1 jalapeño chile, seeded, finely chopped

1 clove garlic, finely chopped

¾ cup finely chopped red onion

¼ cup chopped fresh cilantro

SWORDFISH

½ cup pineapple juice

1 tablespoon grated lime peel

2 tablespoons lime juice

2 tablespoons rum, if desired

1 tablespoon olive or canola oil

1 teaspoon paprika or

¼ teaspoon ground red pepper (cayenne)

2 lb swordfish steaks, cut into 6 serving-size pieces

1 In medium bowl, mix salsa ingredients. Cover and refrigerate until serving time or up to 4 days.

2 Heat gas or charcoal grill. In shallow dish, mix pineapple juice, lime peel, lime juice, rum, the oil and paprika. Place swordfish in dish; let stand at room temperature 10 minutes to marinate.

3 Place fish on grill over medium heat. Cover grill; cook 8 to 12 minutes, turning once, until fish flakes easily with fork. Serve fish with salsa.

1 SERVING: Calories 240; Total Fat 9g (Saturated Fat 2.5g; Trans Fat 0g); Cholesterol 80mg; Sodium 75mg; Total Carbohydrate 12g (Dietary Fiber 2g)

EXCHANGES: 1 Other Carbohydrate, 3½ Lean Meat

CARBOHYDRATE CHOICES: 1

If you can't get swordfish, try another firm-textured fish, such as grouper, halibut, shark or tuna.

Grilled Marinated Shrimp

START TO FINISH 30 MINUTES
4 SERVINGS

½ teaspoon grated lime peel

¼ teaspoon ground cumin

¼ teaspoon dried oregano leaves

⅛ teaspoon salt

2 tablespoons olive or canola oil

2 tablespoons lime juice

2 cloves garlic, finely chopped

1 lb uncooked deveined peeled large shrimp

1 Heat gas or charcoal grill. In medium bowl, mix all ingredients except shrimp. Add shrimp; toss to coat. Let stand at room temperature 10 minutes to marinate.

2 Remove shrimp from marinade; thread loosely onto 4 (12- to 14-inch) metal skewers. Reserve marinade.

3 Place skewered shrimp on grill over medium heat. Cover grill. Cook 3 to 7 minutes, turning once and brushing occasionally with reserved marinade, until shrimp turn pink. Discard any remaining marinade.

1 SERVING: Calories 110; Total Fat 4.5g (Saturated Fat 0.5g; Trans Fat 0g); Cholesterol 160mg; Sodium 220mg; Total Carbohydrate 0g (Dietary Fiber 0g)

EXCHANGES: 2½ Very Lean Meat, ½ Fat

CARBOHYDRATE CHOICES: 0

Salmon with Lemon Butter and Pineapple Salsa

START TO FINISH 20 MINUTES
4 SERVINGS

LEMON BUTTER

1 tablespoon butter or margarine, softened

4 teaspoons grated lemon peel

2 teaspoons lemon juice

PINEAPPLE SALSA

2 cups chopped fresh pineapple

¼ cup chopped fresh cilantro

2 tablespoons finely chopped red onion

1 teaspoon finely chopped jalapeño chile, if desired

SALMON

4 salmon fillets, about 1 inch thick (1½ lb)

¼ teaspoon salt

1 Heat oven to 375°F. In small bowl, mix lemon butter ingredients; set aside.

2 In medium bowl, mix pineapple salsa ingredients; cover and refrigerate until serving time.

3 Line 13x9-inch pan with foil. Place salmon, skin side down, in pan; sprinkle with salt.

4 Bake 8 to 10 minutes or until fish flakes easily with fork. Immediately top salmon with lemon butter. Serve with pineapple salsa.

1 SERVING: Calories 300; Total Fat 13g (Saturated Fat 4.5g; Trans Fat 0g); Cholesterol 120mg; Sodium 270mg; Total Carbohydrate 11g (Dietary Fiber 1g)

EXCHANGES: ½ Fruit, 5 Lean Meat Carbohydrate Choices: 1

If you prefer halibut, go ahead and substitute it for the salmon. Just follow the guidelines for the thickness and weight called for in the recipe.

Pan-Roasted Halibut over Rotini

START TO FINISH 15 MINUTES
4 SERVINGS

2⅔ cups uncooked rainbow rotini pasta (8 oz.)

4 halibut fillets, ½ to ¾ inch thick (4 oz. each), skin removed

1 teaspoon seasoned salt

½ teaspoon coarse ground black pepper

1 Cook pasta as directed on package. Drain; cover to keep warm.

2 Meanwhile, sprinkle both sides of halibut with salt and pepper. Heat 10-inch nonstick skillet over high heat. Immediately place fish in skillet; cook 1 minute or until golden brown.

3 Turn fish; reduce heat to medium. Add ⅓ cup water; cover and cook 5 to 8 minutes or until fish flakes easily with fork. Serve fish over pasta.

1 SERVING: Calories 310; Total Fat 2.5g (Saturated Fat 0g; Trans Fat 0g); Cholesterol 60mg; Sodium 660mg; Total Carbohydrate 45g (Dietary Fiber 3g; Sugars 0g)

EXCHANGES: 3 Starch, 3 Very Lean Meat

CARBOHYDRATE CHOICES: 3

CHAPTER 6

Cakes

AND PIES

Glazed Lemon Pound Cake

START TO FINISH 3 HOURS
16 SERVINGS

CAKE

1 cup butter, softened

2 cups sugar

4 eggs

1 tablespoon grated lemon
  peel

3 cups all-purpose flour

1 teaspoon baking powder

1 teaspoon salt

½ teaspoon baking soda

1 cup milk

GLAZE

⅓ cup sugar

¼ cup lemon juice

2 tablespoons butter

1 Heat oven to 350°F. Generously grease 12-cup fluted tube cake pan with shortening.

2 In large bowl, beat 1 cup butter and 2 cups sugar with electric mixer on medium speed until light and fluffy, scraping bowl occasionally. Add eggs, one at a time, beating well and scraping bowl after each addition. Beat in lemon peel. On low speed, beat in flour, baking powder, salt, baking soda and milk until smooth, scraping bowl occasionally. Pour batter evenly into pan.

3 Bake 45 to 50 minutes or until toothpick inserted near center comes out clean. Cool upright in pan 15 minutes.

4 Meanwhile, in 1-quart non aluminum saucepan, mix glaze ingredients. Heat over medium heat, stirring occasionally, until butter melts.

5 Place serving plate upside down over pan; turn plate and pan over. Remove pan. With long-tined fork or skewer, generously prick top and sides of cake. Brush warm glaze over cake, allowing glaze to soak into cake. Cool completely, about 1 hour 30 minutes.

1 SERVING: Calories 350; Total Fat 15g (Saturated Fat 7g; Trans Fat 1g); Cholesterol 90mg; Sodium 330mg; Total Carbohydrate 48g (Dietary Fiber 0g; Sugars 30g)

EXCHANGES: 1 Starch, 2 Other Carbohydrate, 3 Fat

CARBOHYDRATE CHOICES: 3

Dixie Spice Cake with Caramel Frosting

START TO FINISH 2 HOURS 15 MINUTES
12 SERVINGS

CAKE

2¼ cups all-purpose flour

1¼ cups packed brown sugar

½ cup granulated sugar

1 teaspoon baking soda

½ teaspoon salt

½ teaspoon ground nutmeg

½ teaspoon ground allspice

1 cup buttermilk

⅔ cup shortening

1 teaspoon vanilla

3 eggs

1 cup chopped walnuts or pecans

FROSTING

½ cup butter or margarine

1 cup packed brown sugar

¼ cup milk

3 cups powdered sugar

½ teaspoon vanilla

1 Heat oven to 350°F. Generously grease bottom only of 13x9-inch pan with shortening or cooking spray; lightly flour.

2 In large bowl, beat all cake ingredients except walnuts with electric mixer on low speed until moistened, scraping bowl occasionally. Beat on medium speed 3 minutes, scraping bowl occasionally. Stir in walnuts. Spread batter evenly in pan.

3 Bake 40 to 45 minutes or until top springs back when touched lightly in center. Cool completely, about 1 hour.

4 In 2-quart saucepan, melt butter. Stir in brown sugar. Cook over low heat 2 minutes, stirring constantly. Add milk; cook until mixture comes to a rolling boil. Remove from heat. Gradually beat in powdered sugar and vanilla until smooth. If needed, add a few drops of milk for desired spreading consistency. Spread over cooled cake.

1 SERVING: Calories 670; Total Fat 27g (Saturated Fat 8g; Trans Fat 2.5g); Cholesterol 75mg; Sodium 310mg; Total Carbohydrate 99g (Dietary Fiber 1g; Sugars 79g)

EXCHANGES: 2 Starch, 4½ Other Carbohydrate, 5 Fat

CARBOHYDRATE CHOICES: 6½

To substitute for buttermilk, use 1 tablespoon vinegar or lemon juice plus milk to make 1 cup.

Dixie Spice Cupcakes: Place paper baking cups in each of 24 to 30 regular-size muffin cups. Fill each ⅔ full with batter. Bake at 350°F 20 to 25 minutes. Spread with frosting.

Hazelnut Cake

START TO FINISH 2 HOURS
16 SERVINGS

CAKE

½ cup butter or margarine

2 packages (2½ oz. each) hazelnuts (filberts) or pecans

3 eggs

1½ cups sugar

1 teaspoon vanilla

2 cups all-purpose flour

2¼ teaspoons baking powder

¼ teaspoon salt

GLAZE

½ cup whipping (heavy) cream

1 cup semisweet chocolate chips (6 oz.)

½ teaspoon vanilla

1 Heat oven to 350°F. Lightly grease bottom only of 10-inch spring-form pan with shortening or cooking spray. In 1-quart saucepan, melt butter over low heat; set aside to cool.

2 Reserve 8 whole nuts for garnish. In food processor or blender, process remaining nuts until ground, making about 1⅓ cups. Reserve 1 tablespoon for garnish.

3 In large bowl, beat eggs, sugar and 1 teaspoon vanilla with electric mixer on medium speed 2 to 3 minutes or until thick and lemon colored, scraping bowl occasionally. On low speed, beat in flour, baking powder, salt and ground nuts, scraping bowl occasionally. Continue beating, gradually adding cooled, melted butter until well blended, scraping bowl occasionally (mixture will be thick). Spread batter evenly in pan.

4 Bake 35 to 45 minutes or until toothpick inserted in center comes out clean. Cool in pan 15 minutes. Remove side of pan; run long knife under cake to loosen from pan bottom. Place heatproof serving plate upside down over cake; turn plate and cake over. Remove pan bottom. Cover cake with cloth towel; cool completely, about 30 minutes.

5 In 2-quart saucepan, heat whipping cream just to boiling; remove from heat. Stir in chocolate chips until melted and smooth. Stir in ½ teaspoon vanilla. Spread glaze over top of cake, allowing some to run down side of cake. Sprinkle reserved ground nuts around top edge of cake; arrange reserved whole nuts over ground nuts.

1 SERVING: Calories 340; Total Fat 18g (Saturated Fat 7g; Trans Fat 0g); Cholesterol 65mg; Sodium 160mg; Total Carbohydrate 39g (Dietary Fiber 2g; Sugars 25g)

EXCHANGES: 1 Starch, 1½ Other Carbohydrate, 3½ Fat

CARBOHYDRATE CHOICES: 2½

Applesauce Cupcakes with Browned Butter Frosting

START TO FINISH 1 HOUR 50 MINUTES
24 CUPCAKES

CUPCAKES

1¼ cups granulated sugar

1½ cups applesauce

½ cup butter, softened

2 eggs

2½ cups all-purpose flour

1 teaspoon ground cinnamon

1 teaspoon baking powder

½ teaspoon baking soda

½ teaspoon salt

¼ teaspoon ground nutmeg

FROSTING

½ cup butter (do not use
   margarine)

4 cups powdered sugar

2 teaspoons vanilla

3 to 4 tablespoons milk

1 Heat oven to 350°F. Line 24 regular-size muffin cups with paper baking cups or grease cups with shortening or cooking spray. In large bowl, beat granulated sugar, applesauce, butter and eggs with electric mixer on medium speed until smooth and creamy, scraping bowl occasionally. On low speed, beat in flour, cinnamon, baking powder, baking soda, salt and nutmeg just until well blended, scraping bowl occasionally. Divide batter evenly among muffin cups.

2 Bake 25 to 35 minutes or until toothpick inserted in center comes out clean. Remove from muffin cups. Cool completely, about 30 minutes.

3 In 3-quart saucepan, melt butter over medium heat. Cook 3 to 5 minutes, stirring constantly and watching closely, until butter just begins to turn golden (butter will get foamy and bubble). Remove from heat. Cool 15 minutes.

4 With electric mixer on low speed, beat in powdered sugar, vanilla and enough milk until frosting is smooth and desired spreading consistency, adding 1 or 2 more teaspoons milk, if necessary. Spread frosting on cooled cupcakes (if frosting begins to harden, stir in an additional teaspoon milk).

1 CUPCAKE: Calories 260; Total Fat 8g (Saturated Fat 4g; Trans Fat 0g); Cholesterol 40mg; Sodium 150mg; Total Carbohydrate 44g (Dietary Fiber 0g; Sugars 33g)

EXCHANGES: 1 Starch, 2 Other Carbohydrate, 1½ Fat

CARBOHYDRATE CHOICES: 3

Black Forest Cherry Cake

START TO FINISH 55 MINUTES
12 SERVINGS

CAKE

1 box (1 lb. 2.25 oz.)
  devil's food cake mix with
  pudding

2 tablespoons all-purpose
  flour

1¾ cups water

3 eggs

FILLING AND
TOPPING

1 can (21 oz.) cherry or
  cherry-cranberry pie filling

¾ teaspoon almond extract

1 container (8 oz.) frozen
  reduced fat whipped
  topping, thawed

Maraschino or candied cherry
  and chocolate curls, if
  desired

1 Heat oven to 350°F. Grease 15x10x1-inch pan with shortening or cooking spray. Line with foil, extending foil over short sides of pan; grease foil. In large bowl, beat cake mix, flour, water and eggs with electric mixer on low speed until moistened, scraping bowl occasionally. Beat on high speed 2 minutes, scraping bowl occasionally. Spread batter evenly in pan.

2 Bake 18 to 20 minutes or until cake springs back when touched lightly in center. Remove cake from pan by lifting foil; place on wire rack. Cool completely, about 15 minutes.

3 Meanwhile, in small bowl, mix pie filling and ½ teaspoon of the almond extract.

4 Cut cooled cake in half crosswise to make 2 (10x7-inch) layers; remove foil. Place 1 cake layer on serving platter or tray; spread pie filling mixture over top. Top with remaining cake layer.

5 Stir remaining ¼ teaspoon almond extract into whipped topping. Spread mixture over sides and top of cake. Serve immediately, or loosely cover and refrigerate until serving time. If desired, garnish each serving with maraschino or candied cherry and chocolate curls. Store in refrigerator.

1 SERVING: Calories 290; Total Fat 7g (Saturated Fat 4g; Trans Fat 0g); Cholesterol 55mg; Sodium 360mg; Total Carbohydrate 53g (Dietary Fiber 2g; Sugars 35g)

EXCHANGES: 1½ Starch, 2 Other Carbohydrate, 1 Fat

CARBOHYDRATE CHOICES: 3½

Fudgy Peppermint Truffle Chocolate Cake

START TO FINISH 2 HOURS 20 MINUTES
12 SERVINGS

FILLING

1 cup semisweet chocolate chips (6 oz.)

⅔ cup sweetened condensed milk (not evaporated)

½ teaspoon peppermint extract

CAKE

1 box (1 lb. 2.25 oz.) devil's food cake mix with pudding

1 container (8 oz.) fat-free sour cream

⅓ cup vegetable oil

3 eggs

ICING

¾ cup powdered sugar

1½ oz. cream cheese, softened

1 to 2 tablespoons milk

6 hard peppermint candies, finely crushed

1 Heat oven to 350°F. Grease 12-cup fluted tube cake pan with shortening; lightly flour. In medium microwavable bowl, microwave filling ingredients on High 30 seconds. Stir until melted and smooth (if necessary, microwave 10 to 20 seconds longer); set aside.

2 In large bowl, beat cake ingredients with electric mixer on low speed until combined; beat 2 minutes on medium speed. Spoon batter evenly into pan. Drop spoonfuls of filling over batter, keeping filling away from side of pan.

3 Bake 35 to 45 minutes or until toothpick inserted near center comes out clean and edge begins to pull away from side of pan. Cool in pan on wire rack 10 minutes. Place wire rack upside down over pan; turn rack and pan over. Remove pan. Cool completely, about 1 hour (center of cake may sink slightly during cooling).

4 In medium bowl, beat powdered sugar, cream cheese and 1 tablespoon of the milk with wire whisk until smooth, adding additional milk until desired drizzling consistency. Drizzle icing over cooled cake; sprinkle with crushed candies. Store in refrigerator.

1 SERVING: Calories 450; Total Fat 17g (Saturated Fat 7g; Trans Fat 0.5g); Cholesterol 65mg; Sodium 410mg; Total Carbohydrate 66g (Dietary Fiber 2g; Sugars 48g)

EXCHANGES: 1½ Starch, 3 Other Carbohydrate, 3 Fat

CARBOHYDRATE CHOICES: 4½

A pastry brush is ideal for greasing the grooves of a fluted tube pan.

White Chocolate–Fudge Torte

START TO FINISH 5 HOURS 40 MINUTES
16 SERVINGS

CAKE

16 oz. semisweet baking
  chocolate, chopped

1 cup unsalted butter

6 eggs

TOPPING

1 cup white vanilla baking
  chips, melted

1 cup whipping (heavy)
  cream

1 package (8 oz.) cream
  cheese, softened

⅓ cup powdered sugar

2 tablespoons white crème de
  cacao, if desired

½ cup miniature semisweet
  chocolate chips, if desired

RASPBERRY SAUCE

1 package (10 oz.) frozen
  raspberries in light syrup,
  thawed

1 tablespoon cornstarch

⅓ cup red currant jelly

1 Heat oven to 400°F. Spray 9-inch springform pan with cooking spray. In 3-quart saucepan, melt semisweet chocolate and butter over medium-low heat, stirring constantly, until smooth. Cool completely.

2 Meanwhile, in small bowl, beat eggs with electric mixer on high speed 5 minutes or until triple in volume. Fold eggs into cooled chocolate mixture until well blended. Pour batter evenly into pan.

3 Bake 15 to 20 minutes (cake edges will be set but center will jiggle when moved). Cool completely in pan on wire rack, about 1 hour 30 minutes. Refrigerate until firm, about 1 hour 30 minutes.

4 In heavy 1-quart saucepan, heat white chocolate and 3 tablespoons of the whipping cream over low heat, stirring frequently, until chocolate is melted. In large bowl, beat cream cheese, powdered sugar and crème de cacao with electric mixer on medium speed until smooth. While beating, slowly add white chocolate mixture, beating until smooth, scraping bowl occasionally.

5 In small bowl, beat remaining whipping cream with electric mixer on high speed until stiff peaks form. With rubber spatula, fold into white chocolate mixture; fold in miniature chocolate chips. Spread topping over cake. Refrigerate until firm, at least 1 hour.

6 To prepare sauce, drain raspberries, reserving syrup. Add water to syrup to make ¾ cup. In 1-quart saucepan, mix syrup mixture and cornstarch. Stir in jelly. Cook over medium heat, stirring frequently, until thickened and clear. Stir in raspberries. Refrigerate until cold.

7 Serve dessert with sauce.

1 SERVING: Calories 490; Total Fat 35g (Saturated Fat 21g; Trans Fat 1g); Cholesterol 145mg; Sodium 85mg; Total Carbohydrate 37g (Dietary Fiber 3g; Sugars 32g) • **EXCHANGES:** 1½ Starch, 1 Other Carbohydrate, 7 Fat • **CARBOHYDRATE CHOICES:** 2½

Orange Cheesecake with Raspberry Sauce

START TO FINISH 8 HOURS 15 MINUTES
16 SERVINGS

CRUST

- 1 package (9 oz.) chocolate wafer cookies, crushed
- 6 tablespoons butter or margarine, melted

FILLING

- 4 packages (8 oz. each) cream cheese, softened
- 1⅓ cups sugar
- 4 eggs
- 2 tablespoons orange-flavored liqueur or orange juice
- 1 teaspoon grated orange peel

SAUCE

- 1 package (10 oz.) frozen raspberries in syrup, thawed
- 3 tablespoons sugar
- 1 teaspoon cornstarch

1 Heat oven to 325°F. In medium bowl, mix crust ingredients; press in bottom and 2 inches up side of ungreased 9-inch springform pan.

2 In large bowl, beat cream cheese with electric mixer on medium speed until smooth and creamy. Gradually beat in 1⅓ cups sugar until smooth, scraping bowl occasionally. On low speed, beat in eggs, one at a time, just until blended. Add liqueur and orange peel; beat on medium speed 2 minutes, scraping bowl occasionally. Pour filling into crust.

3 Bake 55 to 65 minutes or until almost set. Cool completely, about 2 hours 30 minutes. Refrigerate at least 4 hours or overnight before serving.

4 In food processor or blender, process raspberries with syrup until smooth. If desired, strain to remove seeds. In 1-quart saucepan, mix 3 tablespoons sugar and the cornstarch. Stir in raspberry puree. Cook over medium heat, stirring constantly, until mixture boils and thickens. Cool to room temperature.

5 Carefully remove side of pan; leave cheesecake on pan bottom. Serve cheesecake with sauce. Store in refrigerator.

1 SERVING: Calories 430; Total Fat 28g (Saturated Fat 16g; Trans Fat 1.5g); Cholesterol 125mg; Sodium 300mg; Total Carbohydrate 38g (Dietary Fiber 1g; Sugars 29g)

EXCHANGES: 2 Starch, ½ Other Carbohydrate, 5½ Fat

CARBOHYDRATE CHOICES: 2½

Use a knife dipped in water to make the smoothest cuts in the cheesecake. And for easier cutting, make the cheesecake 24 to 36 hours ahead of serving and keep it refrigerated.

Apple Pie Foldover

START TO FINISH 1 HOUR 15 MINUTES
4 SERVINGS

FILLING

1½ cups thinly sliced peeled apples (1½ medium)

¼ cup packed brown sugar

1 tablespoon water

1 teaspoon lemon juice

1 tablespoon all-purpose flour

1 tablespoon granulated sugar

¼ teaspoon salt

1 tablespoon butter or margarine

½ teaspoon vanilla

CRUST

1 Pillsbury refrigerated pie crust (from 15-oz box), softened as directed on box

1 egg

1 tablespoon water

1 teaspoon granulated sugar

⅛ teaspoon ground cinnamon

1 In 2-quart saucepan, mix apples, brown sugar, 1 tablespoon water and the lemon juice. Cook over medium heat, stirring occasionally, until bubbly. Reduce heat to low; cover and cook 6 to 8 minutes, stirring occasionally, until apples are tender.

2 In small bowl, mix flour, 1 tablespoon granulated sugar and the salt. Gradually stir into apple mixture, cooking and stirring until mixture thickens. Remove from heat; stir in butter and vanilla. Cool 15 minutes.

3 Meanwhile, heat oven to 375°F. On ungreased cookie sheet, unroll pie crust. Spoon cooled filling evenly onto half of crust to within ½ inch of edge.

4 In small bowl, beat egg and 1 tablespoon water; brush over edge of crust. Fold untopped half of crust over filling; firmly press edge to seal. Flute edge; cut small slits or shapes in several places in top crust. Brush top with remaining egg mixture. In another small bowl, mix 1 teaspoon granulated sugar and the cinnamon; sprinkle over crust.

5 Bake 25 to 35 minutes or until crust is golden brown. Cool on cooling rack at least 10 minutes before serving.

1 SERVING: Calories 380; Total Fat 18g (Saturated Fat 7g; Trans Fat 0g); Cholesterol 70mg; Sodium 410mg; Total Carbohydrate 51g (Dietary Fiber 0g)

EXCHANGES: ½ Starch, 3 Other Carbohydrate, 3½ Fat

CARBOHYDRATE CHOICES: 3½

Tart apples such as Granny Smith or Haralson make flavorful apple foldovers. Braeburn or Gala apples provide good texture and a slightly sweeter flavor.

Orchard Medley Pie

START TO FINISH 3 HOURS 10 MINUTES
8 SERVINGS

FILLING

1½ cups diced peeled apples

¾ cup fresh red raspberries

¾ cup fresh blackberries

¾ cup fresh blueberries

¾ cup chopped rhubarb

¾ cup sugar

3 tablespoons quick-cooking tapioca

1 tablespoon lemon juice

1½ tablespoons cold butter or margarine, cut into small pieces

CRUST

1 box (15 oz) Pillsbury refrigerated pie crusts, softened as directed on box

1 Place foil or cookie sheet on oven rack below middle rack to catch any spills if the filling should bubble over during baking. Heat oven to 400°F. In large bowl, stir together filling ingredients. Let stand 15 minutes, stirring occasionally.

2 Make pie crusts as directed on box for Two-Crust Pie, using 9-inch glass pie plate. Spoon filling into crust-lined pie plate; dot with butter. Top with second crust; seal edge and flute. Cut slits or shapes in several places in top crust. Cover crust edge with foil to prevent excessive browning.

3 Bake 15 minutes; reduce oven temperature to 350°F. Bake 30 to 35 minutes longer or until filling bubbles in slits, removing foil during last 15 minutes of bake time. Cool on cooling rack at least 2 hours before serving.

1 SERVING: Calories 370; Total Fat 16g (Saturated Fat 6g; Trans Fat 0g); Cholesterol 15mg; Sodium 240mg; Total Carbohydrate 56g (Dietary Fiber 2g) Exchanges: 1/2 Fruit, 3 1/2 Other Carbohydrate, 3 Fat

CARBOHYDRATE CHOICES: 4

For a decorative top on your pie, cut off overhang of crust in pie plate to be even with plate edge. Spoon filling into crust-lined pie plate; dot with butter. Cut second crust into 1- to 1½-inch squares using fluted pastry wheel. Place squares over top of pie, pressing edge pieces gently into bottom crust edge. If desired, brush squares with milk and sprinkle with coarse or granulated sugar. Bake the pie as directed.

Individual Mixed-Berry Pies

START TO FINISH 1 HOUR 5 MINUTES
4 PIES

FILLING

1 cup frozen unsweetened whole strawberries, thawed

¾ cup frozen unsweetened blueberries, thawed

¾ cup frozen unsweetened raspberries, thawed

⅓ cup sugar

2 tablespoons cornstarch

CRUST

1 Pillsbury refrigerated pie crust (from 15-oz box), softened as directed on box

1 teaspoon sugar

1 Heat oven to 425°F. In large bowl, mix filling ingredients. Divide filling mixture evenly among 4 (6-oz) custard cups or ramekins.

2 Unroll pie crust on work surface. Cut 4 (5-inch) rounds from pie crust. Place each round over pie filling, draping over edges of custard cups. Cut slits or shapes on top of each. Sprinkle with 1 teaspoon sugar. Place custard cups on cookie sheet.

3 Bake 17 to 23 minutes or until edges are deep golden brown and centers are thoroughly baked. Cool on cooling rack about 30 minutes. Serve warm.

1 PIE: Calories 330; Total Fat 11g (Saturated Fat 4g; Trans Fat 0g); Cholesterol 5mg; Sodium 170mg; Total Carbohydrate 57g (Dietary Fiber 5g)

EXCHANGES: ½ Fruit, 3½ Other Carbohydrate, 2 Fat Carbohydrate Choices: 4

These are great little pies to make during the months when fresh berries aren't at their peak. But during berry season you may want to make them using fresh berries instead of frozen.

Rhu-Berry Pie

START TO FINISH 2 HOURS 10 MINUTES
8 SERVINGS

CRUST

1 box (15 oz) Pillsbury
refrigerated pie crusts,
softened as directed
on box

FILLING

2 cups cut-up fresh rhubarb*

2 cups fresh blueberries*

¾ cup sugar

¼ cup all-purpose flour

⅛ teaspoon ground nutmeg

Dash salt

2 teaspoons milk

1 tablespoon coarse sugar,
if desired

1 Heat oven to 400°F. Make pie crusts as directed on box for Two-Crust Pie, using 9-inch glass pie plate.

2 In large bowl, mix filling ingredients except milk and coarse sugar; toss gently to mix. Spoon into crust-lined pie plate.

3 Unroll second crust on work surface. Cut crust into about 2x1½-inch rectangles. Place in straight rows across filling, placing one corner over the other, leaving about 1 inch between rows. Place remaining dough rectangles around edge, overlapping to fit. Brush with milk; sprinkle with coarse sugar. Cover crust edge with foil to prevent excessive browning.

4 Bake 42 to 46 minutes or until filling bubbles in middle and crust is golden brown, removing foil during last 15 to 20 minutes of bake time. Cool on cooling rack at least 1 hour before serving.

*Two cups cut-up frozen rhubarb and 2 cups frozen blueberries can be substituted for the fresh rhubarb and blueberries.

1 SERVING: Calories 350; Total Fat 14g (Saturated Fat 5g; Trans Fat 0g); Cholesterol 10mg; Sodium 240mg; Total Carbohydrate 54g (Dietary Fiber 1g)

EXCHANGES: 3½ Other Carbohydrate, 3 Fat

CARBOHYDRATE CHOICES: 3½

Get creative with the crust! Instead of rectangles, cut the second crust into shapes using a small cookie cutter to cut hearts, circles or other shapes. Place the shapes across the filling leaving space between each shape. Place any remaining shapes around the edge, overlapping to fit if necessary.

Lemon Mini Tarts

START TO FINISH 25 MINUTES
16 TARTS

1 cup fat-free (skim) milk

1 box (4-serving size) lemon instant pudding and pie filling mix

1 teaspoon grated lemon peel

1 refrigerated pie crust (from 15-oz box), softened as directed on box

Strawberry halves, lemon slices or other fresh fruit

Fresh mint leaves

Powdered sugar, if desired

1 In medium bowl, beat milk and pudding mix 2 minutes with electric mixer at medium speed or 2 to 3 minutes with wire whisk until well blended. Stir in lemon peel. Refrigerate.

2 Heat oven to 450°F. Using rolling pin, roll pie crust to 15-inch diameter. With lightly floured 3-inch round cutter, cut 16 rounds from crust; discard scraps. Fit rounds into 16 (2¾-inch) ungreased muffin cups, pressing in gently. Generously prick crusts with fork. Bake 5 to 7 minutes or until very light golden brown. Remove from pan; cool completely.

3 Spoon lemon filling into tart shells. Garnish with fruit and mint; sprinkle with powdered sugar.

1 TART: Calories 70; Total Fat 2.5g (Saturated Fat 1g; Trans Fat 0g); Cholesterol 0mg; Sodium 135mg; Total Carbohydrate 12g (Dietary Fiber 0g)

EXCHANGES: 1 Other Carbohydrate, ½ Fat

CARBOHYDRATE CHOICES: 1

Turn these into banana cream tarts by using banana instant pudding and pie filling mix and sliced bananas.

Bake and freeze the crusts up to three months ahead.

Chocolate-Pecan Pie

START TO FINISH 2 HOURS 40 MINUTES
10 SERVINGS

CRUST

1 refrigerated pie crust (from 15-oz. box), softened as directed on box

FILLING

1 cup light corn syrup

½ cup sugar

¼ cup butter or margarine, melted

1 teaspoon vanilla

3 eggs

1 cup semisweet chocolate chips (6 oz.)

1½ cups pecan halves

TOPPING

10 pecan halves

½ cup whipping (heavy) cream, whipped

1 Heat oven to 325°F. Using 9-inch glass pie plate, make pastry as directed in recipe or place pie crust in pie plate as directed on box for One-Crust Filled Pie.

2 In large bowl, beat corn syrup, sugar, butter, vanilla and eggs with wire whisk until well blended. Reserve 2 tablespoons chocolate chips for topping; stir remaining chocolate chips and the 1½ cups pecans into corn syrup mixture. Pour into pastry-lined pie plate, spreading evenly. Cover edge with 2- to 3-inch-wide strips of foil to prevent excessive browning; remove foil during last 15 minutes of baking.

3 Bake 55 to 65 minutes or until deep golden brown and filling is set. Cool completely, about 1 hour.

4 Meanwhile, line cookie sheet with waxed paper. In small microwavable bowl, microwave reserved 2 tablespoons chocolate chips on Medium (50%) 1 minute to 1 minute 30 seconds or until melted; stir. Dip each of 10 pecan halves into chocolate; place on cookie sheet. Refrigerate until chocolate is set, 15 to 20 minutes, before serving.

5 Just before serving, top pie with whipped cream and chocolate-dipped pecans. Store in refrigerator.

1 SERVING: Calories 560; Total Fat 34g (Saturated Fat 11g; Trans Fat 1.5g); Cholesterol 90mg; Sodium 210mg; Total Carbohydrate 58g (Dietary Fiber 3g; Sugars 33g)

EXCHANGES: 2 Starch, 2 Other Carbohydrate, 6½ Fat

CARBOHYDRATE CHOICES: 4

French Silk Chocolate Pie

START TO FINISH 3 HOURS
10 SERVINGS

CRUST

1 refrigerated pie crust (from 15-oz. box), softened as directed on box

FILLING

3 oz. unsweetened baking chocolate, cut into pieces

1 cup butter, softened (do not use margarine)

1 cup sugar

½ teaspoon vanilla

4 pasteurized eggs or 1 cup fat-free egg product

TOPPING

½ cup sweetened whipped cream

Chocolate curls, if desired

1 Heat oven to 450°F. Using 9-inch glass pie plate, make pastry as directed in recipe or place pie crust in pie plate as directed on box for One-Crust Baked Shell. Bake 9 to 11 minutes or until lightly browned. Cool completely, about 30 minutes.

2 Meanwhile, in 1-quart saucepan, melt chocolate over low heat; cool. In small bowl, beat butter with electric mixer on medium speed until fluffy. Gradually beat in sugar until light and fluffy. Beat in cooled chocolate and vanilla until blended. Add 1 egg (or ¼ cup egg product) at a time, beating on high speed 2 minutes after each addition; beat until mixture is smooth and fluffy.

3 Pour filling into cooled baked shell. Refrigerate at least 2 hours before serving.

4 Just before serving, top pie with whipped cream and, if desired, chocolate curls. Store in refrigerator.

1 SERVING: Calories 460; Total Fat 34g (Saturated Fat 15g; Trans Fat 2.5g); Cholesterol 140mg; Sodium 270mg; Total Carbohydrate 33g (Dietary Fiber 2g; Sugars 21g)

EXCHANGES: 1 Starch, 1 Other Carbohydrate, 7 Fat

CARBOHYDRATE CHOICES: 2

Pasteurized eggs are uncooked eggs that have been heat-treated. Be sure to use pasteurized eggs or egg product in this recipe since they're not cooked. Pasteurized eggs can be found in the dairy case at large supermarkets.

Banana Split Tart

START TO FINISH 1 HOUR 15 MINUTES
16 SERVINGS

CRUST

1 box (15 oz.) refrigerated pie crusts, softened as directed on box

FILLING

½ cup semisweet chocolate chips, melted

2 containers (6 oz. each) banana crème low-fat yogurt

2 small bananas, sliced

1 can (21 oz.) strawberry pie filling with more fruit

1 cup fresh strawberries, sliced

1 Heat oven to 375°F. Remove pie crusts from pouches; unroll 1 crust in center of ungreased large cookie sheet. Unroll second crust and place over first crust, matching edges and pressing to seal. With rolling pin, roll out into 14-inch round. Fold ½ inch of crust edge under, forming border; press to seal seam. If desired, flute edge. Prick crust generously with fork.

2 Bake 20 to 25 minutes or until golden brown. Cool completely, about 30 minutes.

3 Spread half of the melted chocolate chips evenly over cooled baked crust. Spread yogurt over chocolate. Arrange banana slices on top of yogurt. Spread pie filling evenly over bananas. Arrange strawberries over pie filling. Drizzle remaining melted chocolate chips over top. Cut into wedges to serve. Store in refrigerator.

1 SERVING: Calories 220 (Calories from Fat 80); Total Fat 9g (Saturated Fat 3.5g; Trans Fat 0g); Cholesterol 0mg; Sodium 125mg; Total Carbohydrate 33g (Dietary Fiber 1g; Sugars 17g)

EXCHANGES: 2 Other Carbohydrate, 2 Fat

CARBOHYDRATE CHOICES: 2

To melt the chips, place them in a microwavable bowl. Microwave on High for 45 seconds, then stir until smooth. If needed, microwave another 10 to 15 seconds.

CHAPTER 7

Cookies
AND BARS

Soft-and-Chewy Chocolate Chip Cookies

START TO FINISH 1 HOUR 10 MINUTES
6 DOZEN COOKIES

1¼ cups granulated sugar

1¼ cups packed brown sugar

1½ cups butter or margarine, softened

2 teaspoons vanilla

3 eggs

4¼ cups all-purpose flour

2 teaspoons baking soda

½ teaspoon salt

1 to 2 bags (12 oz. each) chocolate chips (2 to 4 cups)

1 Heat oven to 375°F. In large bowl, beat granulated sugar, brown sugar and butter with electric mixer on medium speed until light and fluffy, scraping bowl occasionally. Beat in vanilla and eggs until well blended. On low speed, beat in flour, baking soda and salt until well combined, scraping bowl occasionally. Stir in chocolate chips.

2 Drop dough by rounded tablespoonfuls 2 inches apart onto ungreased cookie sheets.

3 Bake 8 to 10 minutes or until light golden brown. Cool 1 minute; remove from cookie sheets.

1 COOKIE: Calories 120; Total Fat 6g (Saturated Fat 3g; Trans Fat 0g); Cholesterol 20mg; Sodium 80mg; Total Carbohydrate 16g (Dietary Fiber 0g; Sugars 10g)

EXCHANGES: 1 Other Carbohydrate, 1 Fat

CARBOHYDRATE CHOICES: 1

Chocolate Candy Cookies: Substitute candy-coated chocolate pieces for the chocolate chips.

Chocolate Chunk Cookies: Substitute 1 to 2 bags (11. 5 to 12 oz. each) semisweet or white chocolate chunks for the chocolate chips.

Brown Sugar–Oatmeal Cookies

START TO FINISH 55 MINUTES
2½ DOZEN COOKIES

1¾ cups packed brown sugar

½ cup shortening

½ cup butter or margarine,
  softened

1 teaspoon vanilla

2 eggs

1 cup all-purpose flour

1 cup whole wheat flour

1 teaspoon baking powder

3 cups old-fashioned oats

1 Heat oven to 350°F. In large bowl, beat brown sugar, shortening and butter with electric mixer on medium speed until light and fluffy, scraping bowl occasionally. Beat in vanilla and eggs until well blended. On low speed, beat in all-purpose flour, whole wheat flour and baking powder until well combined, scraping bowl occasionally. Stir in oats.

2 Drop dough by heaping tablespoonfuls 2 inches apart onto ungreased cookie sheets.

3 Bake 10 to 14 minutes or until light golden brown. Cool 1 minute; remove from cookie sheets.

1 COOKIE: Calories 170; Total Fat 7g (Saturated Fat 2.5g; Trans Fat 1g); Cholesterol 20mg; Sodium 45mg; Total Carbohydrate 24g (Dietary Fiber 1g; Sugars 13g)

EXCHANGES: ½ Starch, 1 Other Carbohydrate, 1½ Fat

CARBOHYDRATE CHOICES: 1½

Check your brown sugar often so you'll always be ready to go. If it's gotten hard, just seal it in a plastic bag with an apple wedge for a day or two to soften it, then throw away the apple. Soft, supple and ready to bake!

Oatmeal-Raisin Cookies

START TO FINISH: 45 MINUTES

3½ DOZEN COOKIES

¾ cup granulated sugar

¼ cup packed brown sugar

½ cup butter or margarine, softened

½ teaspoon vanilla

1 egg

¾ cup all-purpose flour

½ teaspoon baking soda

½ teaspoon ground cinnamon

¼ teaspoon salt

1½ cups quick-cooking oats

½ cup raisins

½ cup chopped nuts

1 Heat oven to 375°F. Grease cookie sheets with shortening or cooking spray. In large bowl, beat granulated sugar, brown sugar and butter with electric mixer on medium speed until light and fluffy, scraping bowl occasionally. Beat in vanilla and egg until well blended. On low speed, beat in flour, baking soda, cinnamon and salt until well combined, scraping bowl occasionally. Stir in oats, raisins and nuts.

2 Drop dough by rounded teaspoonfuls 2 inches apart onto cookie sheets.

3 Bake 7 to 10 minutes or until edges are light golden brown. Cool 1 minute; remove from cookie sheets.

1 COOKIE: Calories 80; Total Fat 3.5g (Saturated Fat 1.5g; Trans Fat 0g); Cholesterol 10mg; Sodium 45mg; Total Carbohydrate 10g (Dietary Fiber 0g; Sugars 6g)

EXCHANGES: ½ Other Carbohydrate, 1 Fat

CARBOHYDRATE CHOICES: ½

Stop the raisin rut! Why not use another dried fruit? Try dried blueberries, cherries, cranberries, chopped dates, apricots or figs, or even dried mixed fruit.

Frosted Ginger Cutouts

START TO FINISH: 3 HOURS 20 MINUTES
3 DOZEN COOKIES

COOKIES

1 cup shortening

1 cup molasses

3 cups all-purpose flour

1½ teaspoons baking soda

½ teaspoon salt

½ teaspoon ground ginger

¼ teaspoon ground nutmeg

¼ teaspoon ground cloves

FROSTING

1 package unflavored gelatin

¾ cup water

¾ cup granulated sugar

¾ cup powdered sugar

¾ teaspoon baking powder

1 teaspoon vanilla

1 In large bowl, beat shortening and molasses with electric mixer on medium speed until blended, scraping bowl occasionally. Stir in remaining cookie ingredients until well combined, scraping bowl occasionally. Cover dough with plastic wrap; refrigerate at least 2 hours for easier handling.

2 Heat oven to 350°F. On well-floured work surface, roll out dough with rolling pin to ¼-inch thickness. Cut with floured 2½-inch round cookie cutter; place 1 inch apart on ungreased cookie sheets.

3 Bake 6 to 9 minutes or until set. Cool 1 minute; remove from cookie sheets. Cool completely, about 10 minutes.

4 In 2-quart saucepan, pour gelatin over water; let stand 5 minutes. Stir in granulated sugar; heat over high heat until full rolling boil. Reduce heat to medium; simmer uncovered 10 minutes without stirring (temperature should read 220°F on candy thermometer). Remove from heat. With electric mixer on low speed, beat in powdered sugar until foamy. Add baking powder and vanilla; beat on low speed 5 minutes or until glossy and spreading consistency, scraping bowl occasionally.

5 Spread frosting on underside of each cookie to within ⅛ inch of edge. If desired, decorate cookies. Let stand until frosting is set before storing.

1 COOKIE: Calories 140; Total Fat 6g (Saturated Fat 1.5g; Trans Fat 1g); Cholesterol 0mg; Sodium 100mg; Total Carbohydrate 22g (Dietary Fiber 0g; Sugars 12g)

EXCHANGES: 1½ Other Carbohydrate, 1 Fat

CARBOHYDRATE CHOICES: 1½

Chocolate-Dipped Peanut Butter Fingers

START TO FINISH: 1 HOUR 35 MINUTES
32 COOKIES

1 roll (18 oz.) refrigerated peanut butter cookies

⅓ cup all-purpose flour

8 oz. sweet baking chocolate, broken into squares

1 tablespoon vegetable oil

Finely chopped peanuts and/ or multicolored candy sprinkles

1 Heat oven to 375°F. In large bowl, break up cookie dough. Stir or knead in flour until well blended.

2 Divide dough into 32 equal pieces. Shape each into 2½-inch-long log; place 2 inches apart on ungreased cookie sheets. With knife, make 3 shallow (about ¼-inch-deep) cuts lengthwise in each log.

3 Bake 6 to 8 minutes or until golden brown. Immediately remove from cookie sheets; place on wire racks. Cool completely, about 15 minutes.

4 In microwavable measuring cup, microwave chocolate and oil on High 30 to 60 seconds, stirring every 15 seconds, until smooth. Dip ⅓ of each cookie into chocolate, allowing excess to drip off. Dip into peanuts; return to wire racks. Let stand until chocolate is set before storing.

1 COOKIE: Calories 130; Total Fat 7g (Saturated Fat 2.5g; Trans Fat 0g); Cholesterol 0mg; Sodium 80mg; Total Carbohydrate 15g (Dietary Fiber 0g; Sugars 9g)

EXCHANGES: 1 Other Carbohydrate, 1½ Fat

CARBOHYDRATE CHOICES: 1

Cinnamon Tea Cakes

START TO FINISH 1 HOUR 30 MINUTES
4½ DOZEN COOKIES

COOKIES

½ cup powdered sugar

1 cup butter or margarine, softened

1 teaspoon vanilla

2 cups all-purpose flour

1 cup finely chopped or ground walnuts

½ teaspoon ground cinnamon

⅛ teaspoon salt

COATING

¼ cup granulated sugar

1 teaspoon ground cinnamon

1 Heat oven to 325°F. In large bowl, beat powdered sugar, butter and vanilla with electric mixer on medium speed until light and fluffy, scraping bowl occasionally. On low speed, beat remaining cookie ingredients until well combined, scraping bowl occasionally.

2 Shape dough into 1-inch balls; place 1 inch apart on ungreased cookie sheets.

3 Bake 14 to 16 minutes or until set but not brown. Meanwhile, in small bowl, mix coating ingredients; set aside. Immediately remove cookies from cookie sheets; place on wire racks. Cool slightly, about 3 minutes.

4 Roll warm cookies in coating; return to wire racks. Cool completely, about 15 minutes. Reroll cookies in coating.

1 COOKIE: Calories 70; Total Fat 5g (Saturated Fat 2g; Trans Fat 0g); Cholesterol 10mg; Sodium 30mg; Total Carbohydrate 6g (Dietary Fiber 0g; Sugars 2g)

EXCHANGES: ½ Other Carbohydrate, 1 Fat

CARBOHYDRATE CHOICES: ½

Use a small or mini food processor to grind the nuts. Process them with on-and-off motions into fine pieces, but not until they're ground into powder.

Chocolate Star Gingersnaps

START TO FINISH 1 HOUR 10 MINUTES
4 DOZEN COOKIES

1 cup packed brown sugar

¾ cup shortening

¼ cup molasses

1 egg

2¾ cups all-purpose flour

1 teaspoon baking soda

1 teaspoon ground ginger

1 teaspoon ground cinnamon

¼ teaspoon ground cloves

¼ cup granulated sugar

48 chocolate star candies

1 Heat oven to 375°F. In large bowl, beat brown sugar, shortening and molasses with electric mixer on medium speed until smooth, scraping bowl occasionally. Beat in egg until well blended. On low speed, beat in flour, baking soda, ginger, cinnamon and cloves until well combined, scraping bowl occasionally.

2 Shape dough into 1-inch balls; roll in granulated sugar and place 2 inches apart on ungreased cookie sheets.

3 Bake 7 to 9 minutes or until tops are cracked and edges are set. Immediately press 1 candy in center of each cookie. Cool 1 minute; remove from cookie sheets.

1 COOKIE: Calories 100; Total Fat 4.5g (Saturated Fat 1.5g; Trans Fat 0.5g); Cholesterol 5mg; Sodium 35mg; Total Carbohydrate 15g (Dietary Fiber 0g; Sugars 9g)

EXCHANGES: 1 Other Carbohydrate, 1 Fat

CARBOHYDRATE CHOICES: 1

Chocolate-Hazelnut Biscotti

START TO FINISH 1 HOUR 40 MINUTES
3 DOZEN BISCOTTI

1 cup sugar

½ cup butter or margarine, softened

2 teaspoons vanilla

3 eggs

2⅔ cups all-purpose flour

¼ cup unsweetened Dutch process baking cocoa

2 teaspoons baking powder

¾ cup hazelnuts (filberts), toasted, chopped

½ cup miniature semisweet chocolate chips

2 oz. vanilla-flavored candy coating or almond bark, chopped

1 Heat oven to 350°F. Lightly grease cookie sheet with shortening or cooking spray. In large bowl, beat sugar and butter with electric mixer on medium speed until light and fluffy, scraping bowl occasionally. Beat in vanilla and eggs until well blended. On low speed, beat in flour, cocoa and baking powder until well combined, scraping bowl occasionally. Stir in toasted hazelnuts and chocolate chips.

2 Divide dough in half; shape each into 10-inch log. Place logs 5 inches apart on cookie sheet; flatten each until 3 inches wide.

3 Bake 20 to 25 minutes or until firm when touched in center. Cool on cookie sheet 10 minutes. With serrated knife, cut diagonally into ½-inch-thick slices. Arrange slices, cut side down, on same cookie sheet.

4 Bake 10 minutes. Turn slices over; bake 5 to 10 minutes longer or until cut sides are lightly browned and crisp. Remove from cookie sheet; place on wire rack. Cool completely, about 10 minutes.

5 In small microwavable bowl, microwave candy coating on High 45 seconds, stirring once, until melted and smooth. If necessary, microwave 20 seconds longer. Drizzle over biscotti.

1 BISCOTTO: Calories 130; Total Fat 6g (Saturated Fat 2.5g; Trans Fat 0g); Cholesterol 25mg; Sodium 50mg; Total Carbohydrate 16g (Dietary Fiber 0g; Sugars 8g)

EXCHANGES: ½ Starch, ½ Other Carbohydrate, 1 Fat

CARBOHYDRATE CHOICES: 1

To toast the chopped hazelnuts, spread them on cookie sheet. Bake in a 350°F oven for 8 to 10 minutes, stirring occasionally, until they're golden brown. To remove the skins, roll the warm nuts in a clean kitchen towel.

Fudgy S'more Bars

START TO FINISH: 1 HOUR 35 MINUTES
32 BARS

CRUST

1 cup graham cracker crumbs (12 squares)

½ cup all-purpose flour

¾ cup packed brown sugar

½ teaspoon baking soda

½ cup butter or margarine, softened

TOPPING

4 cups miniature marshmallows

¾ cup candy-coated chocolate pieces

¼ cup hot fudge topping, heated

1 Heat oven to 350°F. Grease 13x9-inch pan with shortening or cooking spray. In large bowl, beat crust ingredients with electric mixer on low speed until coarse crumbs form, scraping bowl occasionally. Press mixture evenly in bottom of pan.

2 Bake 10 to 12 minutes or until golden brown. Sprinkle marshmallows evenly over crust; bake 1 to 2 minutes longer or until marshmallows begin to puff.

3 Sprinkle chocolate pieces evenly over marshmallows; drizzle warm topping over top. Cool completely, about 1 hour. Cut into 8 rows by 4 rows.

1 BAR: Calories 120; Total Fat 4.5g (Saturated Fat 2.5g; Trans Fat 0g); Cholesterol 10mg; Sodium 70mg; Total Carbohydrate 19g (Dietary Fiber 0g; Sugars 14g)

EXCHANGES: 1 Other Carbohydrate, 1 Fat

CARBOHYDRATE CHOICES: 1

Easy Caramel-Pecan Bars

START TO FINISH 2 HOURS 45 MINUTES
36 BARS

1 roll (16 oz) refrigerated
   sugar cookies

¾ cup caramel topping

2 tablespoons all-purpose
   flour

1 cup pecan pieces

1 cup flaked coconut

1 bag (6 oz) semisweet chocolate chips (1 cup)

1 Heat oven to 350°F. Spray 13x9-inch pan with cooking spray. Cut dough into ½-inch-thick slices; arrange in bottom of pan. With floured fingers, press dough evenly to cover bottom of pan. Bake 10 to 15 minutes or until light golden brown.

2 Meanwhile, in glass measuring cup, stir caramel topping and flour until smooth.

3 Sprinkle bars with pecans, coconut and chocolate chips. Drizzle with caramel mixture.

4 Bake 15 to 20 minutes longer or until topping is bubbly. Cool completely, about 1½ hours. For bars, cut into 6 rows by 6 rows.

1 BAR: Calories 14; Total Fat 7g (Saturated Fat 2.5g; Trans Fat 0.5g); Chol esterol 0mg; Sodium 70mg; Total Carbohydrate 18g (Dietary Fiber 0g; Sugars 11g)

EXCHANGES: ½ Starch, ½ Other Carbohydrate, 1½ Fat

CARBOHYDRATE CHOICES: 1

Chocolate Chip–Peanut Butter Bars

START TO FINISH 2 HOURS
36 BARS

BASE AND TOPPING

2¼ cups quick-cooking oats

1¼ cups packed brown sugar

1 cup all-purpose flour

½ teaspoon baking soda

1 cup butter, softened

FILLING

1 can (14 oz.) sweetened condensed milk (not evap- orated)

¼ cup peanut butter

½ teaspoon vanilla

1 cup semisweet chocolate chips (6 oz.)

½ cup coarsely chopped salted peanuts

1 Heat oven to 350°F. Grease 13x9-inch pan with shortening or cook- ing spray. In large bowl, beat base and topping ingredients with electric mixer on low speed until crumbly, scraping bowl occasionally. Reserve 2 cups crumb mixture for topping; press remaining mixture evenly in bot- tom of pan.

2 In small bowl, mix condensed milk, peanut butter and vanilla with spoon until well blended. Pour evenly over base. Sprinkle with choco- late chips and peanuts. Sprinkle reserved crumb mixture over top; press down gently.

3 Bake 25 to 30 minutes or until golden brown (center will not be set). Cool completely, about 1 hour 15 minutes. Cut into 6 rows by 6 rows.

1 BAR: Calories 190; Total Fat 10g (Saturated Fat 4.5g; Trans Fat 0g); Cholesterol 15mg; Sodium 85mg; Total Carbohydrate 23g (Dietary Fiber 1g; Sugars 16g)

EXCHANGES: ½ Starch, 1 Other Carbohydrate, 2 Fat

CARBOHYDRATE CHOICES: 1½

Maple-Walnut Pie Bars

START TO FINISH 2 HOURS 25 MINUTES
36 BARS

1 roll (18 oz.) refrigerated
    sugar cookies

3 eggs

⅓ cup packed brown sugar

2 tablespoons all-purpose
    flour

1⅓ cups maple-flavored syrup

1½ cups chopped walnuts

Powdered sugar, if desired

1 Heat oven to 350°F (325°F for dark pan). In ungreased 13x9-inch pan, break up cookie dough. With floured fingers, press dough evenly in bottom of pan. Bake 13 to 15 minutes or until edges are golden brown.

2 Meanwhile, in large bowl, beat eggs with wire whisk. Stir in brown sugar, flour and syrup until well blended. Stir in walnuts.

3 Pour egg mixture evenly over partially baked crust; bake 30 to 35 minutes longer or until filling is set. Cool completely on wire rack, about 1 hour 30 minutes. If desired, sprinkle with powdered sugar. Cut into 6 rows by 6 rows.

1 BAR: Calories 150; Total Fat 6g (Saturated Fat 1g; Trans Fat 0.5g); Cholesterol 20mg; Sodium 60mg; Total Carbohydrate 20g (Dietary Fiber 0g; Sugars 11g)

EXCHANGES: 1½ Other Carbohydrate, 1 Fat

CARBOHYDRATE CHOICES: 1

Frosted Irish Cream Brownies

START TO FINISH 2 HOURS
48 BROWNIES

BROWNIES

1 box (1 lb 3.8 oz.) fudge brownie mix

½ cup vegetable oil

¼ cup Irish cream liqueur

2 eggs

FROSTING

½ cup butter or margarine, softened

2 cups powdered sugar

2 tablespoons Irish cream liqueur

½ teaspoon vanilla

2 to 3 teaspoons milk

GLAZE

1 oz. semisweet baking chocolate, chopped

1 teaspoon butter or margarine

1 Heat oven to 350°F. Grease bottom only of 13x9-inch pan with shortening. In medium bowl, stir brownie mix, oil, ¼ cup liqueur and the eggs with spoon until well blended. Spread batter in pan.

2 Bake 28 to 30 minutes or until brownies are set and begin to pull away from sides of pan. DO NOT OVERBAKE. Cool completely, about 45 minutes.

3 In small bowl, beat ½ cup butter until light and fluffy. Beat in all remaining frosting ingredients, adding enough milk for desired spreading consistency. Spread over cooled brownies.

4 In small microwavable bowl, microwave glaze ingredients on High 30 seconds; stir until melted and smooth. Drizzle over frosted brownies. Refrigerate until firm, about 30 minutes. For brownies, cut into 8 rows by 6 rows.

1 BROWNIE: Calories 120; Total Fat 5g (Saturated Fat 2g, Trans Fat 0g); Cholesterol 15mg; Sodium 60mg; Total Carbohydrate 16g (Dietary Fiber 0g, Sugars 13g)

EXCHANGES: ½ Starch, ½ Other Carbohydrate, 1 Fat

CARBOHYDRATE CHOICES: 1

Cranberry-Apple Pie Squares

START TO FINISH 2 HOURS 40 MINUTES
12 SERVINGS

CRUST

1½ cups all-purpose flour

1 tablespoon granulated sugar

¼ teaspoon salt

½ cup butter or margarine

1 egg yolk

¼ cup milk

FILLING

8½ cups thinly sliced, peeled baking apples (3 lb.; about 9 medium)

1 cup granulated sugar

¼ cup all-purpose flour

2 teaspoons ground cinnamon

½ teaspoon salt

1 cup chopped fresh or frozen (thawed) cranberries

TOPPING

1 cup all-purpose flour

½ cup packed brown sugar

½ cup butter or margarine, softened

1 cup caramel topping, heated

Vanilla or cinnamon ice cream, if desired

1 Heat oven to 375°F. In large bowl, mix 1½ cups flour, 1 tablespoon granulated sugar and ¼ teaspoon salt. With pastry blender or fork, cut in ½ cup butter until mixture resembles coarse crumbs. In small bowl, beat egg yolk and milk with fork until well blended. Add to flour mixture; stir just until dry ingredients are moistened.

2 On lightly floured work surface, roll dough with rolling pin into 15x11-inch rectangle; place in ungreased 13x9-inch pan. Press in bottom and 1 inch up sides of pan.

3 In large microwavable bowl, microwave apples on High 6 to 8 minutes, stirring every 2 minutes, until apples are fork-tender. Stir in remaining filling ingredients except cranberries until well mixed. Spoon apple mixture over crust. Sprinkle with cranberries.

4 In medium bowl, mix 1 cup flour, the brown sugar and ½ cup butter until crumbly; sprinkle over fruit.

5 Bake 45 to 60 minutes or until topping is deep golden brown, apples are tender and filling is bubbly. Cool 1 hour before serving. Serve topped with caramel topping and, if desired, ice cream.

1 SERVING: Calories 500; Total Fat 17g (Saturated Fat 8g; Trans Fat 1g); Cholesterol 60mg; Sodium 350mg; Total Carbohydrate 83g (Dietary Fiber 4g; Sugars 52g)

EXCHANGES: 1 Starch, 4½ Other Carbohydrate, 3 Fat

CARBOHYDRATE CHOICES: 5½

Pumpkin Pie Squares

START TO FINISH 2 HOURS
12 SERVINGS

CRUST

¾ cup all-purpose flour

¾ cup oats

½ to 1 cup chopped nuts

½ cup butter or margarine, softened

1 box (4-serving size) butterscotch pudding and pie filling mix (not instant)

FILLING

2 eggs

1 cup coconut, if desired

1½ teaspoons pumpkin pie spice

1 can (15 oz.) pumpkin (not pumpkin pie mix)

1 can (14 oz.) sweetened condensed milk (not evaporated)

1 Heat oven to 350°F. In large bowl, mix crust ingredients until well combined. Press mixture evenly in bottom of ungreased 13x9-inch pan.

2 In same bowl, beat eggs with wire whisk. Stir in remaining filling ingredients until blended. Pour over crust.

3 Bake 35 to 45 minutes or until knife inserted in center comes out clean. Cool completely, about 1 hour. If desired, serve topped with whipped cream or ice cream. Store in refrigerator.

1 SERVING: Calories 310; Total Fat 15g (Saturated Fat 6g; Trans Fat 0.5g); Cholesterol 65mg; Sodium 150mg; Total Carbohydrate 38g (Dietary Fiber 2g; Sugars 25g)

EXCHANGES: 2 Starch, ½ Other Carbohydrate, 3 Fat

CARBOHYDRATE CHOICES: 2½

Helpful Nutrition
and Cooking Information

Nutrition Guidelines

We provide nutrition information for each recipe that includes calories, fat, cholesterol, sodium, carbohydrate, fiber and protein. Individual food choices can be based on this information.

Recommended intake for a daily diet of 2,000 calories as set by the Food and Drug Administration

Total Fat	Less than 65g
Saturated Fat	Less than 20g
Cholesterol	Less than 300mg
Sodium	Less than 2,400mg
Total Carbohydrate	300g
Dietary Fiber	25g

CRITERIA USED FOR CALCULATING NUTRITION INFORMATION

- The first ingredient was used wherever a choice is given (such as ⅓ cup sour cream or plain yogurt).

- The first ingredient amount was used wherever a range is given (such as 3- to 3½–pound cut-up broiler-fryer chicken).

- The first serving number was used wherever a range is given (such as 4 to 6 servings).

- "If desired" ingredients and recipe variations were not included (such as sprinkle with brown sugar, if desired).

- Only the amount of a marinade or frying oil that is estimated to be absorbed by the food during preparation or cooking was calculated.

INGREDIENTS USED IN RECIPE TESTING AND NUTRITION CALCULATIONS

- Ingredients used for testing represent those that the majority of consumers use in their homes: large eggs, 2% milk, 80%-lean ground beef, canned ready-to-use chicken broth and vegetable oil spread containing not less than 65 percent fat.

- Fat-free, low-fat or low-sodium products were not used, unless otherwise indicated.

- Solid vegetable shortening (not butter, margarine, nonstick cooking sprays or vegetable oil spread as they can cause sticking problems) was used to grease pans, unless otherwise indicated.

EQUIPMENT USED IN RECIPE TESTING

We use equipment for testing that the majority of consumers use in their homes. If a specific piece of equipment (such as a wire whisk) is necessary for recipe success, it is listed in the recipe.

- Cookware and bakeware without nonstick coatings were used, unless otherwise indicated.

- No dark-colored, black or insulated bakeware was used.

- When a pan is specified in a recipe, a metal pan was used; a baking dish or pie plate means ovenproof glass was used.

- An electric hand mixer was used for mixing only when mixer speeds are specified in the recipe directions. When a mixer speed is not given, a spoon or fork was used.

COOKING TERMS GLOSSARY

Beat: Mix ingredients vigorously with spoon, fork, wire whisk, hand beater or electric mixer until smooth and uniform.

Boil: Heat liquid until bubbles rise continuously and break on the surface and steam is given off. For rolling boil, the bubbles form rapidly.

Chop: Cut into coarse or fine irregular pieces with a knife, food chopper, blender or food processor.

Cube: Cut into squares ½ inch or larger.

Dice: Cut into squares smaller than ½ inch.

Grate: Cut into tiny particles using small rough holes of grater (citrus peel or chocolate).

Grease: Rub the inside surface of a pan with shortening, using pastry brush, piece of waxed paper or paper towel, to prevent food from sticking during baking (as for some casseroles).

Julienne: Cut into thin, matchlike strips, using knife or food processor (vegetables, fruits, meats).

Mix: Combine ingredients in any way that distributes them evenly.

Sauté: Cook foods in hot oil or margarine over medium-high heat with frequent tossing and turning motion.

Shred: Cut into long thin pieces by rubbing food across the holes of a shredder, as for cheese, or by using a knife to slice very thinly, as for cabbage.

Simmer: Cook in liquid just below the boiling point on top of the stove; usually after reducing heat from a boil. Bubbles will rise slowly and break just below the surface.

Stir: Mix ingredients until uniform consistency. Stir once in a while for stirring occasionally, often for stirring frequently and continuously for stirring constantly.

Toss: Tumble ingredients (such as green salad) lightly with a lifting motion, usually to coat evenly or mix with another food.

Metric Conversion Guide

VOLUME

U.S. Units	Canadian Metric	Australian Metric
1/4 teaspoon	1 mL	1 ml
1/2 teaspoon	2 mL	2 ml
1 teaspoon	5 mL	5 ml
1 tablespoon	15 mL	20 ml
1/4 cup	50 mL	60 ml
1/3 cup	75 mL	80 ml
1/2 cup	125 mL	125 ml
2/3 cup	150 mL	170 ml
3/4 cup	175 mL	190 ml
1 cup	250 mL	250 ml
1 quart	1 liter	1 liter
1 1/2 quarts	1.5 liters	1.5 liters
2 quarts	2 liters	2 liters
2 1/2 quarts	2.5 liters	2.5 liters
3 quarts	3 liters	3 liters
4 quarts	4 liters	4 liters

WEIGHT

U.S. Units	Canadian Metric	Australian Metric
1 ounce	30 grams	30 grams
2 ounces	55 grams	60 grams
3 ounces	85 grams	90 grams
4 ounces (1/4 pound)	115 grams	125 grams
8 ounces (1/2 pound)	225 grams	225 grams
16 ounces (1 pound)	455 grams	500 grams
1 pound	455 grams	1/2 kilogram

MEASUREMENTS

Inches	Centimeters
1	2.5
2	5.0
3	7.5
4	10.0
5	12.5
6	15.0
7	17.5
8	20.5
9	23.0
10	25.5
11	28.0
12	30.5
13	33.0

TEMPERATURES

Fahrenheit	Celsius
32°	0°
212°	100°
250°	120°
275°	140°
300°	150°
325°	160°
350°	180°
375°	190°
400°	200°
425°	220°
450°	230°
475°	240°
500°	260°

NOTE: The recipes in this cookbook have not been developed or tested using metric measures. When converting recipes to metric, some variations in quality may be noted.

Index